SERMONS PREACHED II
AND MISSION CO

Don't Forget Your Dream

Artur A. Stele, Editor

BIBLICAL RESEARCH INSTITUTE

REVIEW AND HERALD PUBLISHING ASSOCIATION
SILVER SPRING, MD 20904
2022

Don't Forget Your Dream /
    [edited by] Artur A. Stele
    Seventh-day Adventists—Sermons
    Seventh-day Adventists—Doctrines
    Bible—Study and Teaching
    BX6122.D688 2022

Printed in the U.S.A. by the
Pacific Press Publishing Association
Nampa, ID 83653-5353

ISBN 978-0-925675-47-7

DON'T FORGET YOUR DREAM

EDITOR
Artur A. Stele

MANAGING EDITOR
Marly Timm

BRI STAFF
Elias Brasil de Souza   Yuriem Rodriguez
Clinton Wahlen   Marly Timm
Frank M. Hasel   Nicol Belvedere

COPY EDITOR
William Fagal

INSIDE LAYOUT
Nicol Belvedere

COVER DESIGN
Nicol Belvedere

CONTENTS

CONTRIBUTORS

ELIAS BRASIL DE SOUZA, PH.D.,
Director of the Biblical Research Institute, General Conference of Seventh-day Adventists, Silver Spring, Maryland, USA.

FELIX H. CORTEZ, PH.D.,
Associate Professor of New Testament Literature, Seventh-day Adventist Theological Seminary, Andrews University, Berrien Springs, Michigan, USA.

GANOUNE DIOP, PH.D.,
Director of Public Affairs and Religious Liberty, General Conference of Seventh-day Adventists, Silver Spring, Maryland, USA.

LASZLO GALLUSZ, PH.D.,
Senior Lecturer of New Testament Studies, Newbold College of Higher Education, Bracknell, Berkshire, United Kingdom.

KLEBER D. GONÇALVES, PH.D.,
Director of Global Mission Center for Secular and Postmodern Studies, General Conference of Seventh-day Adventists.

S. JOSEPH KIDDER, D.MIN.,
Professor of Pastoral Theology and Discipleship, Seventh-day Adventist Theological Seminary, Berrien Springs, Michigan, USA.

RICK MCEDWARD, DIS (DOCTOR OF INTERCULTURAL STUDIES),
President of the Middle East and North Africa Union Mission (MENAUM), Beirut, Lebanon.

JIŘÍ MOSKALA, TH.D., PH.D.,
Dean of the Seventh-day Adventist Theological Seminary, Andrews University, Berrien Springs, Michigan, USA.

ÁNGEL MANUEL RODRÍGUEZ, TH.D.,
Retired Director of the Biblical Research Institute, General Conference of Seventh-day Adventists, Silver Spring, Maryland, USA.

ARTUR A. STELE, PH.D.,
General Vice President of the General Conference of Seventh-day Adventists, Silver Spring, Maryland, USA.

ALBERTO R. TIMM, PH.D.,
Associate Director of the Ellen G. White Estate, General Conference of Seventh-day Adventists, Silver Spring, Maryland, USA.

TED N. C. WILSON, PH.D.,
President of the General Conference of Seventh-day Adventists, Silver Spring, Maryland, USA.

INTRODUCTION

ARTUR A. STELE

The International Bible and Mission Conferences (IBMCs) have become a good tradition in the Seventh-day Adventist Church in the last decade. Beginning in early 2011, we have now conducted over 140 Conferences. Though the last two years were impacted by the Coronavirus pandemic, even this could not stop the IBMCs. New ways of electronic delivery have been discovered that have significantly increased the number of participants. In several Divisions not only Church pastors and educators were able to join, but also Church elders. Nobody and nothing can stop the Church from fulfilling its mission to proclaim the biblical truth to the world.

In addition to the many lectures/presentations that were offered at these Conferences, we usually started our days with a devotional and prayer time. Sermons that were presented have proved to be a blessing to our listeners. In the many responses we have received from our dear pastors, many of them mentioned how they were blessed and encouraged through the sermon times.

One of the pastors approached a presenter and shared with him that he had come to this Conference with the sole purpose to see his Conference President and hand him a resignation letter. However, he stated that he was so much encouraged through the messages delivered that he decided to continue serving the Lord. He took his resignation letter and cut it in pieces. It was very rewarding to hear this. Space does not permit me to share more of the positive responses we have received verbally and in writing. This very fact encouraged us to select some sermons preached at the IBMCs and publish them in this book.

The title of this book, "Don't Forget Your Dream," comes from a sermon preached by Dr. Ángel Manuel Rodríguez. In his sermon Ángel presented the dream that God gave to the king of Babylon, recorded in the second chapter of the Book of Daniel. However, as we all well know, the king forgot the particulars of the dream. Many of us who listened to this sermon still remember the applications Dr. Rodriguez made to all his listeners. God has shared His dream with us; He has entrusted His message, His

Word, to us. Do we remember it? Or have we forgotten it? Or even worse, have we replaced it, or simply modified it? Ángel very clearly stated: "To be left on this world without a dream is one of the most severe forms of punishment anyone can experience. Living in this dark world is often a threatening experience; we need a dream! Forgetting God's dream for the human race is the very source of disorientation and of the abundance of pain on this planet. Yes, the human race forgot God's dream for them, but we should never forget the dream." God has a very distinctive dream for us as the Church, and He also has a very special dream for every one of us pastors and Church members. Will we remember the dream?

The book starts with a chapter that presents the keynote address to many of the IBMCs from the General Conference President, Elder Ted N. C. Wilson. Dr. Wilson is the one who in 2010 initiated the IBMCs by requesting the Biblical Research Institute of the General Conference to conduct IBMCs around the world. He titled his presentation, "The Spiritual Life of an Administrator, Pastor, or Church Leader." Here the reader will find twenty areas that strongly affect our spiritual life.

The concluding three chapters of this book are dedicated to the Three Angel's Messages. These chapters come from Dr. Ganoune Diop. Many years has Dr. Diop dedicated to the study of the Book of Revelation. His numerous presentations on the Three Angel's Messages have encouraged many listeners to continue researching and digging deeper and deeper into the text till fresh waters of the Word start freely flowing, rejuvenating and invigorating the reader.

It is our hope that all the sermons presented in this book written and preached by the lecturers of the International Bible and Mission Conferences will become a blessing to the readers and will encourage all of us to keep the dream God has entrusted to us alive. Is God's dream your dream? If so, then please, don't forget your dream!

CHAPTER 1

THE SPIRITUAL LIFE OF AN ADMINISTRATOR, PASTOR, OR CHURCH LEADER

Ted N. C. Wilson

It is not easy to be a church administrator, pastor, or church leader today. To carry out your work and mission according to God's direction takes a strong spiritual connection with Him. It is essential that you maintain this close connection since not only you need to do your work well, but God wants to bless others through the Holy Spirit's work in you and through you.

Seventh-day Adventists have long been known to promote and believe in a balanced approach to life that includes the mental, social, physical, and spiritual aspects of our existence. That means your life as a spiritual administrator is affected by all aspects of activity and must be regulated by your connection with heaven and your following the spiritual and natural laws given by the Lord.

Your spirituality will be determined by your allowing God to control your life and bring biblical principles into your everyday work and personal experiences. The message of Micah 6:8 must permeate your thinking and actions: "He has shown you, O man, what is good; and what does the Lord require of you but to do justly, to love mercy, and to walk humbly with your God?"[1] If you will fulfill the three requirements God outlines, you will be a powerful spiritual administrator and exhibit a strong spiritual life. God asks you to do what is right or just and not to shirk your duty in fulfilling the law through His power. However, you are not to be so rigid in your justice that you forget to apply mercy,

---

[1] Scripture passages are quoted from the New King James Version.

as appropriate, through the leading of the Holy Spirit. Then, God requires you to be humble in your approach to God and your fellow human beings. When you "walk humbly with your God," you will naturally walk humbly with others. You will realize that you do not have all the answers and that only in relying totally on Christ can you effectively lead people in a spiritual way.

As you fulfill Micah 6:8, through God's direct leading in your life you will exhibit the spiritual life that Paul portrays in Colossians 1:9-18, showing that Christ must be central in your life and activities. Paul says,

> For this reason we also, since the day we heard it, do not cease to pray for you, and to ask that you may be filled with the knowledge of His will in all wisdom and spiritual understanding; that you may walk worthy of the Lord, fully pleasing Him, being fruitful in every good work and increasing in the knowledge of God; strengthened with all might, according to His glorious power, for all patience and longsuffering with joy; giving thanks to the Father who has qualified us to be partakers of the inheritance of the saints in the light. He has delivered us from the power of darkness and conveyed us into the kingdom of the Son of His love, in whom we have redemption through His blood, the forgiveness of sins. He is the image of the invisible God, the firstborn over all creation. For by Him all things were created that are in heaven and that are on earth, visible and invisible, whether thrones or dominions or principalities or powers. All things were created through Him and for Him. And He is before all things, and in Him all things consist. And He is the head of the body, the church, who is the beginning, the firstborn from the dead, that in all things He may have the preeminence.

In order for you to be a spiritual administrator, pastor, or leader, you must understand that Christ "is the head of the body" and has preeminence in all things. When you understand this humble respect for our Creator who created us and this world in six literal, consecutive, 24-hour days of recent origin, and you respect Him as the Lord of your life because He justified you through His death on the cross and daily sanctifies you through the indwelling of the Holy Spirit in your life, you can then be used in a powerful way as a spiritual administrator.

The connection with Christ in all you do will have a powerful effect on your influence. The spiritual life of an administrator, pastor, or leader is strongly affected by the following areas:

STUDY OF AND LITERAL BELIEF IN THE WORD OF GOD

You must take time daily to study the Bible and allow the Word to soak into your very being, studying to show yourself approved unto God, as 2 Timothy 2:15 indicates. Your understanding and belief in the Bible must involve a literal acceptance of what it says. Our church has long held to the Historical-Biblical method of interpreting Scripture, allowing the Bible to interpret itself—line upon line, precept upon precept. However, one of the most sinister attacks against the Bible and its doctrines comes from those who follow the Historical-Critical method of explaining the Bible—individuals who are influenced by the unbiblical approach of "higher criticism," which is a deadly enemy of our theology and mission. This approach puts a scholar or individual above the plain approach to the Scriptures and gives inappropriate license to decide what he or she perceives as truth, based on the resources and education of the critic. Stay away from this type of approach. It does not lead people to trust God and His Word and will destroy a correct theology and a correct mission. So, preach the Word, as we are admonished in 2 Timothy 4:2.

28 FUNDAMENTAL BELIEFS OF THE SEVENTH-DAY ADVENTIST CHURCH

Have complete trust in and belief of the 28 Fundamental Beliefs of the church. Know the beliefs and realize that they are based on the Word of God. Stand up for the beliefs and support them. Teach them to others and promote them. They are biblical beliefs. Feed God's sheep the Word of God, as indicated in John 21:17.

COMPLETE TRUST IN AND STUDY OF THE SPIRIT OF PROPHECY

Accept the Spirit of Prophecy as one of God's greatest gifts to His remnant people, the Seventh-day Adventist Church. The Spirit of Prophecy has counsel for nearly every aspect of the Christian life and is just as relevant today as when it was written. They are messages from heaven. Daily read the Spirit of Prophecy.

Believe it. Promote it. Use it. Teach it. Support it. Believe the biblical instruction about the Spirit of Prophecy in Revelation 12:17 and 19:10.

ACTIVE PRAYER LIFE

As an administrator you cannot survive without an active, personal prayer life that puts you in contact with the heavenly source of all wisdom and guidance. Pray in the morning, at noon, at night—all the time. Ask the Lord for guidance as you are counseling people, as you chair a committee, as you give instruction for a project, as you deal with problems, and as you conduct every activity of the day. Without an active prayer life, you will not be a spiritual administrator or have the success God wishes for your work. Believe fully the admonition in 1 Thessalonians 5:17, to "pray without ceasing."

BELIEF IN REVIVAL AND REFORMATION

Realize that we are truly in a Laodicean setting and need revival and reformation through the power of the Holy Spirit. Be willing to humble yourself before God and ask your fellow officers and colleagues to do the same as you seek the power of the latter rain through the Holy Spirit. Realize that we are at the end of time and desperately need the Lord to remake us in His image to bring about revival and reformation in our own lives and in the church. Let Revelation 3:18-20 be fulfilled in your life as you ask God for gold refined in the fire, for a white garment, and eye salve from heaven so that you will allow Christ to come into your own heart.

SHARE YOUR FAITH

Be willing to be used by the Holy Spirit to share your faith personally with those you meet. By doing this you will be strengthening your spiritual life. Be willing to hold public evangelistic meetings, which will not only bring others to a knowledge of Christ and a decision for Him but will increase your own belief in this great Advent movement and our fundamental beliefs. Fulfill the great commission of Matthew 28:19-20.

LIFT UP CHRIST, HIS RIGHTEOUSNESS, AND THE SANCTUARY SERVICE

In your daily personal and work activities, lift up Christ in all you do. Make Christ the focus of your life. Speak often of Him to others. Help your associates and those you come in contact with to realize that only through Christ's ministry during His life, His death on the cross at Calvary, and His ministry as our High Priest in the heavenly sanctuary (as outlined in Daniel 8:14 and the book of Hebrews) can we have full assurance of eternal life. We owe everything to Christ for justification, sanctification, and ultimately glorification. Let your message flow from your personal relationship with Christ and what Peter indicates in 1 Peter 1:17-21.

THE THREE ANGELS' MESSAGES

Proclaim with a loud voice the three angels' messages of Revelation 14:6-12. Realize that the Seventh-day Adventist Church has been given a unique message to proclaim to the world, and we are to do it through the Holy Spirit's power.

HAVE A SUNNY DISPOSITION AND BE A UNIFIER

Be positive in your approach to life. Have a sunny disposition in relation to others. Bring encouragement into their lives. Be part of the solution, not part of the problem. Fulfill Christ's prayer of unity found in John 17. Follow the counsel in 2 Corinthians 5:18-19 to bring reconciliation to those around you.

BE OBSERVANT AND AFFIRMING

In your relationships with others, be observant of their activities and accomplishments. When they have been working hard and have accomplished certain goals, be affirming in your appreciation, thereby bringing them encouragement to do more for the Lord. Remember that you are all part of the Lord's team. Be a fulfillment of Proverbs 15:23 with a word spoken in due season.

TRUST DEEPLY IN GOD'S LEADING

Do not doubt for a moment that God is leading the Seventh-day Adventist Church and the Advent movement. This is not just another denomination; this is a mighty movement of the Lord. Have an abiding trust in the promises of the Scriptures and the Spirit of Prophecy. God will carry His people through to the culmination of the great commission given to His people. God has called the Seventh-day Adventist Church for a unique role of proclaiming the three angels' messages, and the Church will continue to the end of time in its special role of lifting up the true worship of God. The characteristics of God's last-day church are identified in Revelation 12:17 and Revelation 14:12.

PHYSICAL EXERCISE AND PROPER EATING HABITS

Realize that what you eat and drink and how you conduct your physical life (exercise, sleep, rest, recreation) will greatly affect your spiritual life. The moral law and the natural law are closely related, since they were given by God Himself. Take time for proper physical exercise and appropriate rest. Do not wear yourself out. You will be hurting your spiritual life as well. Eat a good vegetarian diet and avoid all harmful beverages and other detrimental habits. God will honor you as He did Daniel. Dare to be a Daniel. Follow the counsel in 3 John 2 that you be in spiritual and physical health.

BE FAIR AND BALANCED

In your dealings with people, be known as one who is fair and balanced in the way you handle situations. Evaluate situations carefully and impartially. Make decisions that are reasonable and based on principles and counsel from the Bible and the Spirit of Prophecy. Let Philippians 4:8 guide your thinking and decision-making.

BE A GOOD LISTENER

A spiritual administrator will learn the art of listening, reserving comments until having heard the "whole" story. Don't jump to conclusions. Wait and listen. Be willing to learn. It is better to have fewer words said and more time spent listening. Fulfill Proverbs 1:5, which indicates that a wise man will hear and increase his learning.

SEEK COUNSEL FROM OTHERS

In your work as a spiritual administrator, ask for counsel from godly people. Do not think you know all the answers. Earnestly seek guidance and instruction from those who know the Lord and whom you therefore trust. Remember that Proverbs 11:14 indicates there is safety in a multitude of counselors.

STAND FOR THE RIGHT

Be willing to stand up for what is right "though the heavens fall," as the book *Education* says on page 57. Do not fear to take a stand for something, even if it is not popular. Allow the Holy Spirit to lead you in forming your opinion and belief. Let the Word of God and the Spirit of Prophecy give you an understanding as to the principle of the matter under discussion. Stand tall for truth in the name of the Lord. Be respectful and honorable as you share what you believe is an appropriate position. Through God's guidance, you too can say what is found in Joshua 24:15, "But as for me and my house, we will serve the LORD."

STAND FOR THOSE WHO CANNOT STAND

Be willing to stand for individuals or causes that have no voice but need to be heard. God will give you guidance as you help those who have little or no access to decision-making. God asks you to be the voice of the widow and the orphan and others who are in need. Follow the ministry of Christ in Luke 4:18.

ASK FOR WISDOM EVERY DAY

Every morning claim James 1:5, asking wisdom from on high for your daily duties. Realize that you are powerless without the wisdom of heaven and complete direction from the Lord. God will give you what you need to accomplish your tasks in being a spiritual administrator.

BE A HUMBLE SERVANT

In your dealings with others, remember that you are God's servant. Allow Micah 6:8 to rule your actions. Remember Proverbs 15:33, which says that "before honor is humility." Fulfill Christ's instruction in Matthew 20:26-28 that whoever would be chief should be a servant. Let us follow Christ's example, Who came to give His life for us. Accept Proverbs 3:7, which tells us, "Do not be wise in your own eyes; fear the Lord and depart from evil."

BELIEVE CHRIST'S COMING IS SOON

Accept and believe in the promises and prophecies that indicate Christ's second coming is imminent. Greater and greater signs indicate that Christ's return is soon. Shape your thinking and actions in accordance with this impelling belief that we are living in the last days of earth's history. Speak about Christ's coming and preach about it. Realize that the descriptions of Christ's return in Matthew 24 and 2 Peter 3 are accurate and true. Believe with certainty the words of Christ recorded in Revelation 22:7: "Behold, I am coming quickly!"

As a Seventh-day Adventist administrator, pastor, or church leader seeking to increase your spiritual connection with heaven for a more effective work at the end of time, commit yourself to following Proverbs 3:5-6, which urges us to "Trust in the LORD with all your heart, and lean not on your own understanding; in all your ways acknowledge Him, and He shall direct your paths."

Realize that the spiritual life of an administrator or church leader must flow out of a deep relationship with Christ and a complete dependence on the power of the Holy Spirit in one's life. In *Selected Messages,* book 2, page 376, we read, "We must have a greater nearness to God. Much less of self and much more of Jesus Christ and His grace must be brought into our everyday life."

As this spiritual connection increases, we will realize our need of Christ more and more. We will understand that our greatest need as spiritual administrators is to plead with God for revival and reformation in our lives and in the life of His church. We will understand more and more what is written in *Selected Messages,* book 1, page 121, which says, "A revival of true godliness among us is the greatest and most urgent of all our needs. To seek this should be our first work." As we come to the end of time, may we truly be God's agents, nurturing revival and reformation through the power of the Holy Spirit, which will bring the latter rain and the coming of the Lord.

In closing, the counsel of God through Peter in 1 Peter 1:13-21 is most helpful to ponder and incorporate into our lives as spiritual administrators for God's church and His people:

> Therefore gird up the loins of your mind, be sober, and rest your hope fully upon the grace that is to be brought to you at the revelation of Jesus Christ; as obedient children, not conforming yourselves to the former lusts, as in your ignorance; but as He who called you is holy, you also be holy in all your conduct, because it is written, 'Be holy, for I am holy.' And if you call on the Father, who without partiality judges according to each one's work, conduct yourselves throughout the time of your stay here in fear; knowing that

you were not redeemed with corruptible things, like silver or gold, from your aimless conduct received by tradition from your fathers, but with the precious blood of Christ, as of a lamb without blemish and without spot. He indeed was foreordained before the foundation of the world, but was manifest in these last times for you who through Him believe in God, who raised Him from the dead and gave Him glory, so that your faith and hope are in God.

May your spiritual life as an administrator, pastor, or church leader constantly increase as you plead with the Lord for revival, reformation, and the latter rain of the Holy Spirit. May your hope grow as you lean completely on Christ who bought you with His precious blood and intercedes for you in the most holy place in preparation for His glorious second return to take us home to heaven. Even so, come, Lord Jesus.

CHAPTER 2

GOD'S COSMIC DREAM FOR HUMANITY

Ángel Manuel Rodríguez

I would like to invite you to come with me to ancient Babylon. It is early in the morning, and soon the light of the rising sun will shine upon the beautiful city. The priests were already active inside the temple, serving the gods of Babylon by changing their clothes and preparing their food—food that would ultimately be placed on the table of the king. The gods would only enjoy the essence of the food. The servants were also active in the palace of King Nebuchadnezzar, ready to please the king. Probably the first servant who saw the king was impacted by his mood. The king's face displayed a concern deeper than usual; he was deeply worried and upset. Soon he ordered that the wise teachers and scientists of Babylon be summoned to the palace for a meeting with him. He had an urgent message for them; in fact, he had an unprecedented request for them. Let us stand in the back of the room and observe what was taking place.

DO NOT FORGET THE DREAM!

The proud scientists walked into the room well-dressed, exuding confidence. The king's speech was short and to the point:

"Last night I had a dream."

The wise men smiled, anticipating that the king wanted them to interpret the dream. They were experts in the interpretation of dreams, and some of them had written books on the topic; archaeologists have found some of these. Then the king added:

"I do not remember the details of the dream. I have forgotten the dream!"

We can sympathize with the king because we too have had dreams, and we too have forgotten them. A forgotten dream could leave us in state of sadness and even disorientation. In fact, to be left on this world without a dream is one of the most severe forms of punishment anyone can experience. Living in this dark world is often a threatening experience; we need a dream! Forgetting God's dream for the human race is the very source of disorientation and of the abundance of pain on this planet. Yes, the human race forgot God's dream for them, but we should never forget the dream.

The king forgot his dream, and this was extremely disturbing to him. God's dream provides a reason for our existence and defines who we are and the final destination of our journey on this planet; yet humans forgot it. What do people do when they forget such an important dream? They do what the king did.

The king concluded that the solution to his predicament was found in human wisdom. His wise men, he thought, should be able to reconstruct his dream. The scholars came in with their dignified looks, their analytical questions, their keen observational skills. Hands went up; the wise men were competing among themselves. They wanted to inform the king that forgetting a dream was a common human experience, that humans have dreams and that it was natural for them to forget their dreams. They assured him that there was absolutely nothing wrong with his experience, at least nothing to be afraid of or to be overly concerned about. Dreams come and go because that is the very nature of a dream. No dream is worth holding to, because new dreams will come to us.

The king was not satisfied with this psycho-social approach to his problem. He demanded that they reconstruct his dream for him. He probably thought that perhaps during the process of reconstruction he could remember or recapture his dream. Was not human wisdom supposed to uncover true knowledge by exploring the unknown, providing the stuff out of which our dreams of the future come into existence?

The wise men were bewildered. How could they reconstruct the dream of the king? This was not a rational request. The king's dream could not be recreated in a laboratory or retrieved from its original source, because its Origin was beyond human control.

Perhaps for the first time in his life the king, who had always been surrounded by wise advisors, realized the limits of human wisdom. This was for him a most threatening experience. He had no one to rely on; he was left alone in this world without his dream. The king was lost in the vastness of his kingdom, living a meaningless existence, without anyone to help him, experiencing only the present. A minister who forgets God's dream for the human race will find himself or herself in that same state of disorientation and confusion, drifting in an ocean of conflicting views, tossed by the waves of chaos from one side to the other, destined to extinction.

As we look at the scene, we know what the protagonists did not know. The king's dream is about a picture, a cosmic picture larger than himself and all of his wise men. It is the most beautiful picture that humans could dream about. It is a picture that provides meaning to human history and to our roles within it. It is a picture of a cosmic journey back to perfect harmony and peace in the universe of God. The picture that we see is indeed a dream for the king, but for us it is the shape of the future. The king needs this dream, and so do we, God's end-time remnant. It is indeed a glorious and magnificent dream of salvation and cosmic restoration. We should never forget this glorious dream!

Human wisdom is unable to grasp the totality of history from beginning to end and to provide a particular goal to it. Humans only have parts of the puzzle but not enough pieces to apprehend the whole picture. We need a dream! Humans live in frustration because they have no answer for the most fundamental question, the one of our existence. Without God's dream for us, we exist gasping for wisdom, with many unresolved issues, in darkness, living in a state of almost constant frustration. We should never forget the dream!

Frustrated by the response of the wise men, the king was ready to bring human wisdom to an end by killing them. This was a drastic solution, which was not a solution at all. The realization of the limits of human wisdom could lead to a rejection of its value, limited as it is. At that moment it is tempting to find refuge in agnosticism or pluralism. The king concluded that if knowledge could not bring certainty, then who needs it?

But among the wise men there were also individuals who had divine wisdom and who had kept the dream—the divine plan for the human race—alive in the midst of the Babylonian confusion. Now they, God's instruments, were threatened by a man who had forgotten his dream and who had discovered the limits of human wisdom. When the dream is forgotten, the life of the dreamers is seriously threatened. It was precisely at such a time that God intervened in a special way to reveal the dream again to the king.

Salvation came through God's wisdom, and through it the dream of the king was reconstructed and explained. Only God could reconstruct a dream of the future for us, because He alone has the power to transform it into reality. Salvation is through God's wisdom!

We see Daniel announcing the intervention of God's wisdom in our world to deliver us from the uncertainties that are corroding our existence. But we also see that same wisdom shaping itself within history in the form of a human being. We hear Paul saying, "We proclaim Christ crucified, a stumbling block to the Jews and foolishness to Gentiles, but to those who are called, . . . Christ the power of God and the wisdom of God" (1 Cor 1:23-24, NRSV). He demonstrated that the dream of the king was real and that in Him the kingdom of God was already here. Do not forget the Dream!

There may be forces within the church suggesting that we should forget the dream because it is a relic from the 19th Century. To them we should say, "Do not forget the dream!"

But this is not the end of the story.

DO NOT MODIFY THE DREAM

We do not know how soon it happened, but we do know that the king decided to create his own dream, rejecting God's wisdom. He modified God's dream of the future and created or at least attempted to define his own view of the future. He decided to modify the dream by rejecting aspects of it that he did not like and by incorporating into it his own view of the future. The result of such radical alteration of the dream was fundamentally a nightmare. The rejection of truth results inthe incorporation of lies into the dream, and a new world picture is offered to the human race as if it were from God, when in reality it is the invention of the creature itself, a corruption of the original. But today I tell you: Do not dare to modify the dream!

Now everyone was forced to accept this new vision of the future and to worship it. Those who dared to reject it were to be thrown into the furnace of fire. It is surprising to observe that the rejection of the king's new dream seems to bode the same result that forgetting God's dream would bring, namely, the threatening of human existence. This is the approach of the enemy: If unable to make them forget the dream, force a new dream upon them. This is the threat that the church constantly faces, and that is essentially a call to forget the dream—because a distortion of the dream is in fact the formulation of a new dream and the rejection of God's dream for us. We should never modify the dream or alter it. This was the temptation the Christian church faced, and the dream was modified and changed.

The king's dream is transmuted into an object of adoration. Now the conflict was between a false object of worship and the true One. The issue was no longer wisdom but power to save from the destructive forces of fire. The king, the originator of this new dream, had the power to take life, to destroy it. The question was whether the Originator of the true dream had the power to preserve life by overcoming the power of the king. When humans take God's revelation and distort it, there is always the danger of intolerance and oppression grounded on religious and political convictions. It becomes an oppressive idol because it is perceived as the only structure through which we can create a meaningful existence. But such things are simply human structures whose walls, sooner or later, will crack and fall.

Yet, the threat for those who are unwilling to accept an altered version of the dream was very real. We all know by personal experience that the furnace of fire is real. We have been there! Paul says that every person who serves the Lord will suffer persecution (2 Tim 3:12). This is not just a personal experience but also a collective one. We are not fighting against human flesh but against the powers of evil that rejoice in bringing disruption into our lives and into the life of the church with the intention of upsetting our relationship with the Lord. It is in those moments of conflict that we raise our silent voices to heaven and, like Christ, ask, "My God, why have you abandoned me?" We seem to be experiencing God's forsaking. But we must never forget the dream or modify it, because according to it the Lord will never leave us alone.

Right there, in Babylon, God had His servants who were unwilling to accept a distorted dream. We see them inside the furnace of fire, feeling the uncomfortable heat of the fire and fearing its constant threat to their fragile lives. Do not modify the dream! The Lord was powerful enough to deliver them! They were delivered in a strange way. God could easily have quenched the fire by bringing torrential waters out of the ground. He could have sent a powerful wind to blow awaythe source of the fire. But He did something else; something much more difficult to do. We see Him in the midst of the fire, accompanying the servants of the Lord and protecting their lives. While in there, they did not hear His voice. He came down to the heat, to the fire silently; He also felt the heat but in the process brought deliverance, salvation. The Lord did not promise you that in your ministry you will never be inside a furnace, but He promised us all something more meaningful. He promised to join us inside it, in order to preserve our fellowship with Him. The threat of human fire is not powerful enough for us to modify the dream, separating us from the Lord. Let us not modify the dream!

It was this same presence of the Lord that closed the mouths of the lions when Daniel, unwilling to accept an altered version of the dream, was cast into the lions' den. It was not that the lions were not hungry. It was God's presence with Daniel among the lions that saved him from death. Daniel must have been very much afraid as he was taken to the lions' den; his emotional pain must have been real. While in the den he may have wondered, "Could it be that they are not yet hungry, but that in a couple of hours they will look at me and say to each other: 'Supper time'? Or, is it the Lord who is here with me, preserving me in the midst of this anguish?" We detect here the reality of uncertainty. At times you may wonder about the presence of God in your ministry, but the truth is that the Lord will never abandon those who do not forget or modify His dream for the human race. The lions could not destroy

Daniel because right in front of them was the Lion of the tribe of Judah.

The angel spoke to a young girl: "You will conceive in your womb and bear a son, and you will call him Jesus, the Savior, the one whom the prophet called Emmanuel" (cf. Luke 1:31; Matt 1:23). Christ joined us in our misery and pain, but this time the beasts attacked Him, the fire "burned" on Him, and the result was salvation. The furnace took the shape of a cross! He never forgot or modified the dream! He followed without the slightest deviation God's plan for Him.

PROCLAIM THE DREAM

The king was not the only one who had a dream; Daniel, too, had one. But it was more than a dream—it was a vision, an unprecedented vision of the future: "In the first year of Belshazzar king of Babylon Daniel saw a dream and visions in his mind as he lay on his bed; then he wrote the dream down" (Dan 7:1, NASB). He wrote the dream down to keep it alive, to make it impossible for humans to claim that they forgot it. He wrote the dream down in order for us to proclaim it to the human race at the close of the cosmic conflict. We are not to forget or modify the dream, but instead we are called by God to proclaim it to every nation, people, and tongue. Daniel's dream was not about beasts with unlimited destructive power threatening the existence of the human race. No, the dream was not about chaos. Who wants to dream about chaos! His dream announced the triumph of good over evil and the establishing of justice and love on our planet. It is a dream about cosmic salvation, and all we have to do is proclaim it.

Yes, the forces of chaos may threaten God's people and may even dare to speak against the Lord Himself, but the prophet's dream is about God's unshakable kingdom (Dan 7). Salvation comes through the defeat of God's enemies, but this is accomplished by God Himself. In God's dream the work of deliverance is exclusively His work. In the dream the imagery used throughout a large section of Daniel 7 was military. There was war. Yet, interestingly, the defeat of the fourth beast and its little horn takes place in the court of law. That is to say, their final destruction has a legal foundation; it is not an arbitrary decision motivated by divine irrational rage.

The divine council is in session; objective evidence is analyzed and used in the decision process. Salvation in this case is the result of judgment and consists in the vindication of God's people and the extermination of the evil power that upset the cosmic order established by God. The Kingdom, handed over by God to the Son of Man, belongs now to Him and to His people. Proclaim the dream!

In the visions of Daniel, judgment, cleansing, and deliverance are almost inseparable. This cluster of ideas is found in Daniel's second dream (Dan 8). He addressed the topic of salvation using a term in which legal, cultic, and soteriological ideas interact (8:14). Through the ideology of the Day of Atonement, Daniel was informed that cosmic order would be restored through judgment, vindication, and cleansing. Salvation was now directly associated with the concept of cleansing, suggesting that there was moral and spiritual dirt that needed to be removed from the universe. The military images of Daniel 7 were left behind, and a new image was used to define that from which the universe needed to be delivered: uncleanness. This brings the issue of salvation home, to a personal level, because it implies that we are unclean. The threat to God's people was no longer an external attack from enemy forces but an internal condition. This was part of the divine dream in that it identified our personal condition and the need for cleansing.

The idea introduced in Daniel 8 is developed in Daniel 9. In his prayer the prophet dealt openly with this internal disease that is a threat to the covenant relationship. This contaminating agent, this hot virus, is called by Daniel "sin" (9:5), and it expresses itself through rebellion, disobedience, and treason. This disease creates in the individual a false sense of security and strengthens his or her pride, the hubris ("arrogance"). But in reality, it is a state of uncleanness, separating the individual from the Lord. How can we be delivered from this condition? Daniel says it is through God's forgiving grace. Therefore, he prayed for forgiveness for himself and for his people. But this was a very costly manifestation of grace, as is made clear through the Messianic prophecy recorded in Daniel 9:24-27.

In the dream/vision, the angel told Daniel that the Anointed One would come bringing forgiveness, cleansing, and righteousness, but that in the process He would die. In fact, according to Isaiah 53 and the New Testament (e.g., John 1:29), cleansing is possible because the Servant of the Lord took on Himself the uncleanness of the world. What a wonderful dream! Salvation consists of the removal of the contaminating agent called sin from the human heart and from the universe. In the case of evil forces, their sin is removed through their extermination. The consummation of the cleansing of God's people and of the universe will result in the restoration of cosmic harmony. Daniel's dream in chapter 8 is pointing to this glorious event, which under God's providence happens to be the very goal of the plan of redemption and of human history. We can already anticipate the consummation of salvation; Michael, the Great Prince, is about to arise (Dan 12:1). The dream is being transmuted into reality; proclaim it!

CONCLUSION

God's dream for the human race is about a salvation that encompasses our individual needs as well as the cosmic ones. It includes God's concern for us by delivering us from the frustrating limits of human wisdom, providing for us a wonderful vision, a dream that we should never forget. It is about our willingness to reject a distorted view of God's dream for us, knowing that in our daily confrontation with pain and suffering He will accompany us, providing for us the strength we need in the midst of the fire or among the lions.

Yes, it is a dream of cosmic proportions that we should continue to proclaim. It is about a salvation that brings cosmic deliverance through judgment and cleansing. Through Christ, uncleanness is removed; atonement is a reality. There are no longer any barriers between God and us, and if you feel that there is one, I have good news for you: the Prince, the Messiah, brought us unlimited cleansing from sin. The dream is about the cleansing power of the cross that restores personal and cosmic peace and harmony.

I anticipate with great eagerness the full realization of the dream of the king and of Daniel. For now, do not forget the dream, do not modify the dream; proclaim it with the power of the Spirit!

CHAPTER 3

DANIEL: A MASTER WITNESS FOR GOD

Félix H. Cortez

Daniel did not perform powerful miracles as Elijah did or preach compelling evangelistic sermons as Peter did. Nevertheless, the faithfulness and wisdom he displayed in his life brought kings and subjects alike to know and trust the God of Israel. If the conversion of Paul, chief of sinners, is the greatest conversion in the New Testament, the conversion of Nebuchadnezzar, king of Babylon and personification of Lucifer's pride (Isa 14:4-21), is perhaps the greatest evidence in the Old Testament of God's power to transform people. I will suggest four lessons we can learn from the life and ministry of Daniel.

EFFECTIVE WITNESSES ARE FAITHFUL

First, God's most powerful witnesses are forged in the crucible of the crises of God's people. It is through the fire of ordeals, beaten with doubt and temptation, that God's witnesses are softened, molded, and tempered to God's honor and glory.

Daniel was born at the most critical moment in the history of Israel in the Old Testament. He was probably born between 623 and 621 b.c.,[1] six years after Josiah began religious reforms in Judah, four years after God called Jeremiah to the prophetic ministry, within one or two years of the finding of the book of the law, and thirty-six years before the destruction of Jerusalem and the temple. Likely of royal lineage,[2] Daniel grew up in the midst of a national conversation about the contents and meaning of the

---

[1] See Jacques Doukhan, *Secrets of Daniel* (Nampa, ID: Pacific Press, 2000), 23, n. 2.

[2] Josephus, *Antiquities.* 10.186.

book of Deuteronomy in the context of the powerful messages of Jeremiah, Zephaniah, Nahum, and Habakkuk. When Nebuchadnezzar conquered Jerusalem in 605, Daniel was hand-picked to be taken captive to Babylon.

It was at this moment that Daniel came to his personal crisis. As he journeyed in bondage to the land of his captivity, Daniel "resolved in his heart" to be faithful to God; yet Daniel's name was changed to celebrate a pagan deity, and it is possible that he was castrated.[3] I wonder whether Daniel ever doubted God's love, his grace, his power, or his wisdom. As a fellow human being, I think that at some moment he did. Yet, he remained faithful. Our God does not call us to witness for him when it makes sense in terms of our personal experience, but when He needs it. He does not demand that we are convincing or even credible. He only asks us that we are faithful.

EFFECTIVE WITNESSES WIN FAVOR

Daniel's resolve to be faithful was tested very soon in the most difficult way, in the little things that are apparently nonessential.[4] Daniel's decision "not to defile himself with the king's food" (Dan 1:8)[5] had both physical and spiritual implications;[6] but, how do you refuse a gift graciously given without insulting the giver? Were issues of food important to the extent of risking offending the king? "In the life of the true Christian [however,] there are no nonessentials; in the sight of Omnipotence every duty is important."[7]

Daniel's request and behavior toward the king's official deserves careful reflection. He was humble. He requested to be allowed not to defile himself, and his explanation for the request did not come across as preposterous or arrogant. Daniel was also sensitive to the difficult position in which he was putting

---

[3] Doukhan, 16.

[4] Ellen G. White, *Prophets and Kings* (Mountain View, CA: Pacific Press, 1917), 488.

[5] Unless otherwise indicated, Scripture quotations are from the English Standard Version (ESV).

[6] See *The Seventh-day Adventist Bible Commentary*, ed. Francis D. Nichol, rev. ed., vol. 4 (Washington, DC: Review and Herald, 1976),760, on Dan 1:8

[7] White, Prophets and Kings, 488.

Ashpenaz and suggested a course of action that would protect him. His goal was not to win an argument but an ally, and that is what he got. Daniel's example shows the true nature of a "righteous person."

We often associate righteousness and wisdom with separation and isolation. We tend to think of wise men as living in the world of books, absorbed in thought, and righteous people absorbed in prayer, as if wisdom and righteousness suffered from extensive contact with the mundane. But Daniel was not an ascetic. Daniel was handsome (Dan 1:4). His food and physical regime did not make him emaciated but "better in appearance and fatter in flesh" (Dan 1:15). He had an erect form, a firm, elastic step, a fair countenance, untainted breath, and undimmed senses.[8] Intellectually he had no match. Daniel was not a spiritual nerd or a religious bore. The Bible says that he was "skillful in *all wisdom*" (Dan 1:4, emphasis supplied). His instruction required the learning of three languages and several disciplines, including natural history, astronomy, mathematics, medicine, myth, and chronicle.[9]

Daniel was socially adept as well. The Bible says that Daniel was "competent to stand in the king's palace" (Dan 1:5). This refers to the "proper manner, poise, confidence, and knowledge of social proprieties" that Daniel had, which equipped him to serve at the royal court.[10] As holy and smart as Daniel was, he knew how to care for his body, dress well, enjoy a good meal, share a good laugh, and make people comfortable. Daniel showed us that physical and social appeal do not clash with smarts and holiness. The best testimony is that which wins favor without compromising the integrity of its message.

EFFECTIVE WITNESSES ARE PART OF A TEAM

As great and talented as Daniel was, he was not a one-man force for God. At that crucial time for the nation, God did not call one man but at least six. All of them worked in different

---

[8] White, Prophets and Kings, 485.

[9] Doukhan, 17; John E. Goldingay, *Daniel*, Word Bible Commentary 30 (Dallas: Word, 1989), 16.

[10] Leon Wood, *A Commentary on Daniel* (Grand Rapids, MI: Zondervan, 1973), 33, quoted in Stephen R. Miller, Daniel, The New American Commentary 18 (Nashville: Broadman & Holman, 1994), 61.

ways, fulfilled different functions, and ministered to different audiences, but all worked under God's coordination. Though vastly different, they collaborated with and respected each other. For example, Daniel studied with care and reflected on the prophecies of Jeremiah (Dan 9:2). Ezekiel reflected on and used the life of Daniel as an example of righteousness and wisdom (Eze 14:14, 20; 28:3). This is especially significant when we realize that Daniel was a world-recognized expert in the sacred language, wisdom, and traditional lore of the Chaldeans, whose pagan practices Ezekiel strongly denounced (Eze 8:14). I am afraid that in the polarized world in which we live, Daniel's education and position would have been more than enough to disqualify his ministry, but Ezekiel was able to look beyond them. Effective witnesses for God do not question God's wisdom in calling those who are different from them but rejoice in the manifold ways God uses to advance his kingdom.

EFFECTIVE WITNESSES ARE PATIENT

Daniel was patient as God worked on the king. The conversion of Nebuchadnezzar took many years and God's direct intervention to come to fruition. At the beginning of their personal relationship, as a result of the king's dream, Daniel testified to the king that there was "a God in heaven who reveals mysteries" (Dan 2:28). When Daniel revealed the dream and its interpretation, Nebuchadnezzar was overwhelmed with the truth of the superiority of the God of Daniel. His confession, however, was not an expression of faith. It was quite ambiguous, in fact. It left the door open to say that *Daniel's god was in fact his own god as well*.

The next confrontation came at the fiery furnace. Overwhelmed once again by God's intervention in favor of Daniel's three friends, Nebuchadnezzar recognized publicly that the God of Israel was in fact "the Most High God" (Dan 3:26-30). There was still a big step, however, between recognizing the superiority of Israel's God and trusting or loving Him. *It was their God, not his God* (Dan 3:28).

The breakthrough came in the third and last round. Nebuchadnezzar dreamed about a huge tree in the middle of the earth that was chopped down. He was alarmed but, significantly, did not call Daniel to interpret the dream. Perhaps, deep in his heart, he knew what the true interpretation was but fought against it. Finally, when no remedy was left, Daniel was summoned, but the king explained that Daniel was called Belteshazzar, "after the name of *my* god" (Dan 4:8).

Nebuchadnezzar heard the warning and restrained himself for a time but was not transformed. A year later, the sentence was fulfilled. "The warfare against self is the greatest battle that was ever fought. The yielding of self, surrendering all to the will of God, requires a struggle; but the soul must submit to God before it can be renewed in holiness."[11] After seven years of living like the beasts (Dan 4:31-33), when Nebuchadnezzar had come to the end of his rope, out of the dark pit of madness, from the dust of his animal abode, he looked up and reached out to the God of heaven. It was a kind of resurrection. He came out of the ordeal transformed, and his first impulse was to praise God: "It has seemed good to me to declare the signs and wonders that the Most High God has done *for me*" (Dan 4:2, emphasis added). Nebuchadnezzar was finally transformed. He had traveled a long road. The God of Daniel was now his own God, and his first impulse was to announce to others what Daniel's God had done *for him*. Nebuchadnezzar had been born as a missionary in the kingdom of God.

No person is able to produce this kind of transformation. Collaborating with God in bringing others under the lordship of Jesus is not simply a duty but a privilege we have. It provides us with a front-row seat to the spectacular exhibition of God's love and grace. May the experience of Daniel be ours as well.

---

[11] Ellen G. White, *Steps to Christ* (Mountain View, CA: Pacific Press, 1892), 43.

CHAPTER 4

THE GOD OF MOSES: WHAT HE CAN DO WHEN WE LET HIM

Jiří Moskala

THE MOST IMPORTANT THING IN LIFE

God is for us and never against us. He accepts people as they are, but He does not want to leave them as they are. He wishes to change them by the power of His grace, Word, and Spirit. We are going to study what God can do in us when we let Him. The example of such a transformation is Moses. However, when reflecting on the life of this servant of the Lord, we will focus on his Lord, the God of Moses, what He can accomplish in our lives.

From time to time, I like to ask Bible students a trivia question: "Where did God lead Israel after He liberated them from Egypt?" Their typical answers are: "God brought them to the Promised Land," "to Mount Sinai," "to the desert." These answers are geographically correct, but thelogically completely wrong. God actually answers this question, which may surprise many. God powerfully states: "'You yourselves have seen what I did to Egypt, and how I carried you on eagles' wings and **brought you to myself**'" (Exod 19:4, emphasis added).[1] Thus, the biblical-theological answer to the question reveals God's priority and goal: "The Lord brought them to Himself."

The living God of the Bible is the God of relationships. What is most important for our Lord is not a thing or even accomplishing an agenda, but a person. Thus, God pays close attention to people, and the primary purpose of His activities is to rebuild a personal relationship with humans. He leads people to places so that,

---

[1] Unless otherwise indicated, Scripture quotations are from the New International Version.

through this journey, He may bring them to Himself. At the end of the Book of Lamentations, Jeremiah longs for this kind of personal relationship with God: "Restore us to yourself, O Lord, that we may be restored!" (Lam 5:21, ESV). All prophets in unison call people to this meaningful personal relationship as, for example, Joel proclaims: "'Even now,' declares the Lord, 'return to me with all your heart, with fasting and weeping and mourning'" (Joel 2:12; see also Ezek 11:19-20, 18:30-32; Hos 14:1). Jesus Himself stated the same: "'And I, when I am lifted up from the earth, will draw all people to myself'" (John 12:32, ESV). God is interested not only in our ethical behavior, right doctrine, or a set of proper actions, but above all in having a personal, intimate relationship with us. Both of the biblical creation accounts (Genesis 1-2) are about *relationship*: the first about the vertical with God (the Sabbath), and the second underlining the horizontal relationship among humans (marriage). The knowledge of God must be an experiential and relational knowledge that leads to salvation (John 17:3).

MOSES AS A MODEL OF GROWTH AND TRANSFORMATION

As recorded in the Gospel according to Exodus 19-34, the story of Moses is very instructive of how God desires to transform our lives. How did God build a relationship with this outstanding leader? How was Moses transformed, and how did he grow to be such a powerful changer and mover of things?

Believers are fascinated by the biblical story of Moses' shining face, but they have a very simplistic understanding of this experience. They assume that God called Moses to Mount Sinai, and after he spent some time with the Lord he returned to camp, and his face was shining. This scenario is just not true. So, what really happened? Let's carefully study Moses' experience.

It is significant to observe that prior to arriving at Mount Sinai, Moses was used by God in a mighty way when the Lord was preparing him for a special leadership role. God gave him the best education, first by his mother, and then in the Egyptian University with top educators and mentors. He was probably put in charge of different military campaigns and learned how to lead people into action. In the land of Midian, while he was taking care of sheep, God used him to write two books: Job and

Genesis.[2] Then in the dramatic event of the burning bush, he was called by God to lead Israel out of Egypt. He saw the defeat of the Egyptian gods and the mighty Egyptian army in the Red Sea. He observed how God for many weeks led Israel from Egypt to Sinai. And after the transforming experience resulting in his shining face, he led Israel for another 39 years to the brink of the Promised Land. The biblical message states that Moses was a faithful servant of God (Deut 34:5; Josh 1:1), an unimpaired light in the darkness, a model prophet against whom others would be measured (Deut 18:15, 18). He was an agent of change, even though the people did not always follow his directions and words. When they did, they prospered.

We may learn from Moses' experience, because his exceptional life story tells us what God can do when we let Him change us. So, how did it happen that Moses' face was radiant?

THE FIRST CLIMB

One reads about Moses' *first encounter* with the Lord on Mount Sinai as follows: "Then Moses went up to God, and the Lord called to him from the mountain and said, 'This is what you are to say to the descendants of Jacob and what you are to tell the people of Israel'" (Exod 19:3). God told him that He wanted to establish a covenant with Israel in order for them to be His special people, a kingdom of priests, and a holy nation (19:5-6). It is revealing that after Moses' descent there is not one word in the text about his radiant face: "So Moses went back and summoned the elders of the people and set before them all the words the Lord had commanded him to speak" (Exod 19:7). People reacted to God's initiative positively: "'We will do everything the Lord has said'" (Exod 19:8).

THE SECOND AND THIRD CLIMBS

For the *second time*, Moses climbed Sinai when he brought Israel's "answer back to the Lord" (Exod 19:8b). God spoke to him (Exod 19:10-13), and then he descended the mountain (Exod 19:14). Again, there is no statement regarding his face being radiant. Later Moses ascended Mt. Sinai for a *third time*: "The Lord

---

[2] See Ellen G. White, "Moses," *Signs of the Times*, February 19, 1880. See also Ellen G. White Comments in *The Seventh-day Adventist Bible Commentary*, 3 (Washington, DC: 1954), 1140.

descended to the top of Mount Sinai and called Moses to the top of the mountain. So Moses went up" (Exod 19:20). God spoke to Him (Exod 19:21-24), and "Moses went down to the people and told them" (Exod 19:25). Even after the third time of being in the Lord's presence, his face was not shining.

A diligent student of the Bible who knows that Moses's face will be radiant on a future day needs to ask a pertinent question: What was it in the life of Moses that caused this new experience? In the past, I thought that Moses' face was radiant because he had been in the presence of the Lord. This assumption proved to be incorrect because the biblical text reports that he had already been in the presence of the Lord several times, and still his face was not shining. So, what would bring about the difference?

According to Exodus 20, God decided to speak to all the people (not only to Moses) when He uttered the Decalogue on Sinai. It was the most solemn occasion in the history of God's people when God Himself spoke in the midst of lightning, music, smoke, and the earthquake. God's voice was heard, and the people were terrified: "When the people saw the thunder and lightning and heard the trumpet and saw the mountain in smoke, they trembled with fear. They stayed at a distance and said to Moses, 'Speak to us yourself and we will listen. But do not have God speak to us or we will die'" (20:18-19). Moses firmly responded: "'Do not be afraid. God has come to test you, so that the fear of God will be with you to keep you from sinning'" (20:20). God wanted to help them by this extraordinary event to cultivate His holy presence in life and to stay connected with Him and follow His instruction, but unfortunately, the people failed to do so.

THE FOURTH CLIMB

After God spoke from Sinai to the people, the Lord invited Moses for the *fourth time* to climb the mountain: "The people remained at a distance, while Moses approached the thick darkness where God was" (Exod 20:21). During this stay on Sinai, God gave Moses the Covenant Code—the interpretation of the Decalogue outlining how to put God's will into social practice (see Exod 20:22–23:33). Moses descended and "went and told the people all the LORD's words and laws," and the people of Israel responded with one voice: "'Everything the LORD has said we will do'" (Exod 24:3). The next day a solemn renewal of the covenant occurred, with the people again stating in nearly the same words that "We will do everything the LORD has said; we will obey," and Israel's relationship with God was even sealed with sacrifices and the sprinkling of the blood (24:5-8).

THE FIFTH CLIMB

After this firm reestablishment of the covenant with God, Moses climbed Sinai for the *fifth* time. At the beginning of this climb, Moses was not alone. He had the excellent company of 73 Israelite leaders: "Moses and Aaron, Nadab and Abihu, and the seventy elders of Israel went up and saw the God of Israel. Under his feet was something like a pavement made of lapis lazuli, as bright blue as the sky. But God did not raise his hand against these leaders of the Israelites; they saw God, and they ate and drank" (Exod 24:9-11). For the leaders, this was the pinnacle experience: they saw God (theophany), and twice the text underlines this reality. It was the time for the leaders to seal the covenant with God by eating together, by a banquet with the Lord, the God of Israel, who was their Host. These leaders were deeply honored by God.

In the Middle East during biblical times (and to a certain extent today), eating together is a high experience, a great honor, and a privilege. It offers forgiveness and forms a bond of friendship, forming one family. It implies being for each other and staying together in times of crisis and problems. By eating together, they promise to each other without words that if something should happen to one party, the other is obliged to come and help. To be invited to a meal was a special treat that was not extended to everyone. To refuse an invitation to the table was the worst kind of insult. This insight helps one to understand the stories in the New Testament where Jesus Christ was heavily criticized for eating with sinners (Luke 5:30). When believers celebrate the Lord's Supper, they also establish this close bond of being for each other while God's actual family is reestablished (see Matt 26:26-30; Mark 14:22-25; 1 Cor 11:23-29).

Excursus: An insight from the lives of Nadab and Abihu, the two sons of Aaron, is very troubling. As sons of Aaron, they were priests. Even though they had such a deep experience with God on Mount Sinai, they were not transformed by this encounter with Him, but they took it as a pretext for superiority and freedom to do what they wanted and liked. They were not growing in knowledge and service but became proud. They should have been shining lights, but their arrogance was their downfall. They became drunk and went with forbidden fire into the Tabernacle. They had seen God, but still their faces were not radiant. On the contrary, their faces were pale because they were found dead in the Tabernacle of God (Leviticus 10:1-2, 9). They became possessors of truth, pleased with themselves, manipulators of holy things, and the holy became common to them. There is a warning here: one can see the Lord, have a great experience with Him, and still be spiritually dead by not allowing Him to change one's own life.

While Moses was on the Mountain of God with the elders, God extended a special invitation to him:

"'Come up to me on the mountain and stay here, and I will give you the tablets of stone with the law and commands I have written for their instruction.' . . . When Moses went up on the mountain, the cloud covered it, and the glory of the Lord settled on Mount Sinai. For six days the cloud covered the mountain, and on the seventh day the LORD called to Moses from within the cloud. . . . Then Moses entered the cloud as he went on up the mountain. And he stayed on the mountain forty days and forty nights" (Exod 24:12, 15-16, 18).

God invited Moses to come closer than anyone else to Him. One can observe how Moses was drawn into a more intimate relationship with the Lord and grew spiritually. Careful reading of the biblical text reveals it: First Moses climbed the mountain and "went up to God" (Exod 19:3), then he went "to the top of the mountain" (Exod 19:20), afterward he approached the cloud, "the thick darkness" in which God resided (Exod 20:21), but now "Moses entered the cloud" where God was, and he stayed with the Lord 40 days and 40 nights. During these 40 days, God gave Moses two precious gifts: (1) the gift of the Decalogue written by God Himself on the two tablets, also chiseled by Him (Exod 24:12), and (2) the instructions on how to build and furnish the Tabernacle (see Exod 25-31).

After spending forty days and forty nights with the Lord, Moses returned to the people. Was his face shining? On the contrary, Moses's face was burning with anger, because he had to confront the Golden Calf apostasy and the people's brash immorality: "When Moses approached the camp and saw the calf and the dancing, his anger burned and he threw the tablets out of his hands, breaking them to pieces at the foot of the mountain" (Exod 32:19). Breaking the tablets of the Decalogue was an external sign of breaking its content. However, God lightly rebuked Moses for it, because later He commanded Moses to chisel two tablets to replace the "two stone tablets . . . which you broke" (Exod 34:1)) so God could again write the Ten Words.

THE SIXTH CLIMB

Terrible things happened in the Israelite camp as a result of their apostasy: many people died due to their rebellion. The following day, Moses declared to the people: "'You have committed a great sin. But now I will go up to the LORD; perhaps I can make atonement for your sin'" (Exod 32:30). It is reported that "Moses went back to the LORD and said, 'Oh, what a great sin these people have committed! They have made themselves gods of gold. But now, please forgive their sin—but if not, then blot me out of the book you have written'" (Exod 32:31-32). So, Moses climbed Mt. Sinai for the *sixth* time. No wonder Moses is considered to be a type of Christ because of his intercessory prayer for sinners and his willingness to offer his own life for them. What exemplary compassion for transgressors! He demonstrated his total dedication to the Lord and sacrificial love for people. The book of Exodus does not say how long Moses stayed this time with the Lord on the Mount, but the book of Deuteronomy reveals that he was on Sinai again for 40 days (see Deut 9:18).

After such commitment, would his face be radiant? Surprisingly, not yet, even though he had already twice spent 40 days with His Lord! So, we ask, what was still missing? In what area did Moses need to grow even more?

THE TENT OF MEETING

At this point, God advised Moses that he did not need to climb Mt. Sinai to meet Him. He instructed him to build a Tent of Meeting, which was constructed outside of the camp. Do not confuse it with the Tabernacle, which was erected later at the center of the Israelite camp. The biblical passage reads:

> Now Moses used to take a tent and pitch it outside the camp some distance away, calling it the 'tent of meeting.' Anyone inquiring of the LORD would go to the tent of meeting outside the camp. And whenever Moses wentout to the tent, all the people rose and stood at the entrances to their tents, watching Moses until he entered the tent (Exod 33:7-8).

I do not know how many times Moses went to the Tent of Meeting to encounter his God, whether it was five, ten, twenty, or even more times. But one thing I know: Moses and the Lord developed a special relationship, a friendship. The text underlines it: "The LORD would speak to Moses face to face, as one speaks to a friend" (Exod 33:11a). A friend is a person to whom you can tell everything, and he or she will always love you, never reject you, and will keep a secret. A friend is present in time of need, available in the time of crisis.

One day when Moses was in discussion with his Friend, he realized that he actually needed to know Him better. The more he knew his Lord, the more he realized that he did not know Him. According to Exodus 33:13, Moses had requested: "'If you are pleased with me, **teach me your ways** so I may know you and continue to find favor with you'" (emphasis added). The knowledge Moses desired was not a mere intellectual understanding of God, but an experiential knowledge of His Person. Up to this time, Moses knew his God very closely. He was the One who inspired him; He was the Almighty God who smashed all the Egyptian gods; He was the Mighty Warrior who opened the Red Sea; He was the Splendid General who defeated the Egyptian army; but He was also the loving and caring Parent who provided for Israel's every need; He was the Revelator of truth and His law. But Moses desired to gain new insights. Please, "teach me your ways," Moses requested from God. He felt that there was much more to learn. He wanted to understand Him better, discover His ways. He knew he did not know everything. No surprise that Moses was characterized as "a very humble man, more humble than anyone else on the face of the earth" (Num 12:3). Even a great leader can be a humble person when he/she knows his/her dependency, has a sense of insufficiency, and a need for learning and collaboration. Moses was teachable.

During that discussion with the Lord, Moses made a special request: "'Show me your glory'" (Exod 33:18), and God's answer was affirmative: "'I will cause all **my *goodness*** to pass in front of you'" (Exod 33:19, emphasis added). From this juxtaposition of words, one can safely conclude that God's glory is His goodness, that the glory of God is His character.[3] The fact is that only God's goodness may change people's thinking and behavior (Rom 2:4), and this was also true for Moses.

THE SEVENTH CLIMB

Before Moses climbed Mt. Sinai for the *seventh time*, God instructed him to chisel two stone tablets so He could again write on them the Decalogue, and Moses obeyed: "So Moses chiseled out two stone tablets like the first ones and went up Mount Sinai early in the morning, as the LORD had commanded him; and he carried the two stone tablets in his hands" (Exod 34:4). Then the Lord revealed His nature to Moses. He "came down in the cloud and stood there with him and proclaimed his name, the Lord" (Exod 34:5). Then the prophet heard the best description of God's character, given by God Himself. The Lord proclaimed that He is "'the compassionate and gracious God, slow to anger, abounding in love and faithfulness, maintaining love to thousands, and forgiving wickedness, rebellion and sin. Yet he does not leave the guilty unpunished; he punishes the children and their children for the sin of the parents to the third and fourth generation" (Exod 34:6-7).

This is the most splendid portrayal of who God is, provided by God Himself. The Lord's nature is presented with His several indispensable attributes. The God of Moses is a God of love, compassion, grace, patience, faithfulness, forgiveness, truth, and justice. This self-revelation of God is the masterpiece of God's revelation that is like a golden thread going through the entire Bible (see, for example, Num 14:18; Neh 9:17; Ps 86:15, 103:8; Joel 2:13; Jonah 4:2). Later biblical authors repeated after God

---

[3] See also Ellen G. White, *The Acts of the Apostles* (Mountain View, CA: Pacific Press, 1911), 576; White, *Christ's Object Lessons* (Washington, DC: Review and Herald, 1900), 414; White, *Prophets and Kings* (Mountain View, CA: Pacific Press, 1917), 313.

and interpreted what the Lord said. It is the John 3:16 of the Hebrew Scriptures. God proclaimed that He is the Lord, namely the close personal God, God of the covenant, God of His people, who intervenes in human affairs and cares for us in order to help us in our troubles. It is plainly confirmed that God's glory is His character of love, because He is love (Deut 7:8, 33:3; John 3:16-1 John 4:8). He is the holy and just God. In the Book of Revelation, the first message begins with God's grace: "Grace to you and peace" (1:4), and the last message ends with a strong wish: "The grace of our Lord Jesus Christ be with you all" (22:21, NKJV).

In this context it is significant to mention that the first and last sentences in *The Great Controversy* series written by Ellen G. White refer to God's love: "'God is love.' 1 John 4:16. His nature, His law, is love. It ever has been; it ever will be,"[4] and "From the minutest atom to the greatest world, all things, animate and inanimate, in their unshadowed beauty and perfect joy, declare that God is love."[5] Her bestseller book *Steps to Christ* begins with the same emphasis: "Nature and revelation alike testify of God's love."[6]

At the time of this seventh ascent, Moses' stay lasted again 40 days: "Moses was there with the Lord forty days and forty nights without eating bread or drinking water. And he wrote on the tablets the words of the covenant—the Ten Commandments" (Exod 34:28). Now for the third time, Moses has spent 40 days and nights on Sinai with the Lord. On returning, after 40 days with God, Moses' face was finally radiant. Yes, at last! The inspired Word declares: "When Moses came down from Mount Sinai with the two tablets of the covenant law in his hands, he was not aware that his face was radiant because he had spoken with the LORD" (Exod 34:29).

Note wisely that Moses did not realize that his face was shining. Those people who shine do not know that they are shining! The closer one is to the Lord, the more keenly that person is aware of his or her imperfections in comparison to God's holiness. Ellen G. White powerfully confirms:

---

[4] Ellen G. White, *Patriarchs and Prophets* (Washington, DC: Review and Herald, 1890), 33.

[5] Ellen G. White, *The Great Controversy* (Mountain View, CA: Pacific Press, 1911), 678.

[6] Ellen G. White, *Steps to Christ* (Mountain View, CA: Pacific Press, 1892), 9.

Those who are really seeking to perfect Christian character will never indulge the thought that they are sinless. Their lives may be irreproachable, they may be living representatives of the truth which they have accepted; but the more they discipline their minds to dwell upon the character of Christ, and the nearer they approach to His divine image, the more clearly will they discern its spotless perfection, and the more deeply will they feel their own defects. When persons claim that they are sanctified, they give sufficient evidence that they are far from being holy. They fail to see their own weakness and destitution. They look upon themselves as reflecting the image of Christ, because they have no true knowledge of Him. The greater the distance between them and their Saviour, the more righteous they appear in their own eyes.[7]

Through this growing and transforming experience, Moses became stronger and more powerful in changing his world. For 39 years, he led God's people through their wilderness experience amid many dangers and challenges from within and from outside.

SECRET TO BECOMING A SPIRITUAL LEADER AND WORLD CHANGER

This leads us back to our principal question that we need to reflect upon: What was it in Moses' life that brought about this change so that His face was radiant? It was not the fact that he was in the presence of God! However, it was important for Moses to go and be in the company of God, because if he had not been in His presence, his face would never shine! It was only when he understood and experienced God's loving, kind, and good character and completely opened himself up to God that Moses was transformed.

This observation is disturbing: it is not enough to be with the Lord and come into God's presence. It is much more important **to know God's goodness existentially** and to open oneself personally to Him, His love, and to the influence of His kindness. Then our hearts and minds can experience a change, and our lives can be transformed. Thus, we should be like a flower opening up to the sunbeam's warmth. Remember that the amazing grace

---

[7] Ellen G. White, *The Sanctified Life* (Washington, DC: Review and Herald, 1889), 7-8.

of God is always transforming. If God's grace does not transform, that means it's not amazing.

While pastoring in Europe years ago, I met two families who for more than 10 years did not speak to each other, even though they were going Sabbath after Sabbath into God's presence in the same church. If we want to be God's instruments of change, we need to allow God to transform us. Only people transformed by God's kindness can transform for good. When we reflect God's character and demonstrate integrity, honesty, and transparency, then we will have a positive power of influence. His characteristics will then be our characteristics. His virtues and attitudes will be ours. We will become like Him. This means we'll be loving as He is loving, as gracious as He is gracious, as forgiving as He is forgiving, as serving as He is serving, as unselfish as He is unselfish, as encouraging as He is encouraging, as patient as He is patient, as faithful as He is faithful. As Ellen G. White has so eloquently stated: "It is the glory of God to give His virtue to His children. He desires to see men and women reaching the highest standard."[8] His glory is to embrace repentant sinners[9] and supply everything that is needed to change them. His glory is to give.[10] For us it means "to reveal His character in our own" character, "and thus make Him known."[11] This reflection of God's character, His goodness, kindness, and tender love must be seen in our actions. In this way, we not only have a chance to be a blessing to the world but also to be a shining light to the whole universe, as Paul states: "For it seems to me that God has put us apostles on display at the end of the procession, like those condemned to die in the arena. We have been made a spectacle to the whole universe, to angels as well as to human beings" (1 Cor 4:9). This cosmic dimension gives our lives and service an outstanding depth and breadth.

---

[8] White, *The Acts of the Apostles*, 530.

[9] White, *Prophets and Kings*, 668.

[10] Ellen G. White, *The Desire of Ages* (Mountain View, CA: Pacific Press, 1898), 21.

[11] Ellen G. White, Manuscript 16, 1890; Ellen G. White Comments, in *The Seventh-day Adventist Bible Commentary* (Washington, DC: Review and Herald, 1957), 979.

TRANSFORMATIONAL RELATIONSHIP

In Christ we are a new creation (2 Cor 5:17), and the apostle Paul explains twice how the transformation of our lives occurs:

- It is experienced by accepting God's mercy: "I appeal to you therefore, brothers, by the mercies of God, to present your bodies as a living sacrifice, holy and acceptable to God, which is your spiritual worship. Do not be conformed to this world, but **be transformed** by the renewal of your mind, that by testing you may discern what is the will of God, what is good and acceptable and perfect" (Rom 12:1-2, ESV, emphasis added). He explains that the change in life occurs first in our mind, and then is reflected in the ethics of our everyday behavior.

- It happens by beholding the beauty of Christ's character. The apostle Paul underlined this truth when he reflected on the experience of Moses' shining face and wrote to Christians: "And we all, with unveiled face, beholding the glory of the Lord, **are being transformed** into the same image from one degree of glory to another. For this comes from the Lord who is the Spirit" (2 Cor 3:18, ESV, emphasis added).

It is interesting that the same word *metamorfoō* is also used for the **transfiguration** of Jesus (Matt 17:2; Mark 9:2; the Greek word is used only these four times in the New Testament as shown above).

The transformation of mind and life is like the metamorphosis of a caterpillar into a beautiful butterfly. This renewal is a daily process in which we need to grow: "Therefore we do not lose heart. Though outwardly we are wasting away, yet inwardly we are being renewed day by day" (2 Cor 4:16, NIV). Peter aptly underlines: "But grow in the grace and knowledge of our Lord and Savior Jesus Christ" (2 Pet 3:18, ESV). This growth and transformation is accomplished only by God's Spirit (Ezek 11:18-20; 36:25-28).

CONCLUSION

On a gloomy day, a father and son visited a cathedral. While they were looking at the stained-glass windows with beautiful depictions of different biblical scenes, the sun suddenly began shining through the glass picture of some standing people, who were suddenly brightly illuminated with impressive light. The small boy asked his father, "Daddy, who are these people?" The father didn't know much about Christianity, Christ, or His disciples, but he quickly replied, "These people are Christians." This dazzling picture stayed in the mind of the son. Later, one day the boy's teacher asked in class, "Children, do you know who Christians are?" The boy remembered the bright picture in the cathedral and answered, "I know—Christians are shining people." Jesus stimulated his followers by stating, "'Let your light shine before others, that they may see your good deeds and glorify your Father in heaven'" (Matt 5:16). Only shining people can be agents of change.

God's love and goodness alone can transform lives. Uniquely, God's kindness leads His followers to be kind, good, and unselfishly serving, as He is kind, good, and unselfish. Even small acts of kindness can change the world. You never know which deed will do so. Your random but systematic and (maybe most of the time) unnoticed tiny postive actions, encouraging words, gestures, or a small incident of compassion may motivate and encourage people in so powerful a way that it can really make you a leader of change.

Maybe we will not change the world, but we can make a difference for good to those immediately around us and contribute to a positive view of life by listening, visiting, playing with, or writing little notes to others in need. We can share God's love with people and in places where there is hatred, peace where there are tensions and miscommunication, understanding and support where there is abuse and pain, and joy where people experience depression and disappointment. Changed individuals warm the people around them and melt the ice in their hearts, and these, in turn, also become loving people.

We can be broken, yet God's grace may restore, heal, and transform us to be reflectors of His goodness and to be efficient contributors to the beauty and meaning of life. Then we will warm people with the love of God, and our lives will become our message. We will not even need to use many words, because through our life we will be preaching Christ. Let's be genuine, consistent, and contagious Christians.

A spiritual power stronger than an atomic bomb is needed to break and transform the human heart. Every change is extremely difficult, for we naturally resist change; we love the *status quo*. Real change cannot be commanded but is experienced as a consequence of being with the Lord, walking daily with Him (Micah 6:8). The God of Moses can transform our life to be as shining as was Moses' life. God Himself makes world-changers. He can do marvelous things in and through us, when we allow Him.

CHAPTER 5

BEHOLD THE LAMB

Artur A. Stele

The Lamb and the blood provide the foundation for the sanctuary service. Genesis 22 provides a depth of knowledge relating to the Sacrifice, Atonement, and Substitution![1]

In Genesis 21:12-13, Abraham was told to send Ishmael away, and now, in chapter 22, he is told to give Isaac back to the Lord. In both cases he rose early in the morning to fulfill the call. In fulfilling these calls Abraham was actually saying goodbye to his future, to all of his hopes and dreams. But it goes even further.

It is of interest to note that there are obvious connections between not only chapters 21 and 22 as stated above, but also between chapters 22 and 12. In both chapters God calls upon Abraham, and Abraham hears two distinct and very challenging, if not "strange," calls.

There are linguistic, grammatical, and thematic connections between these two passages, these two calls.

First, in both places an unusual Hebrew expression for "go" is used: *lek leka*. It is used only in chapter 12:1 and chapter 22:2! The reader or the listener could not do otherwise but to connect these two passages because of thisunique phrase. It rang like an alarm, bringing to memory the only other place where this phrase was also used.

Secondly, the grammar in both places is similar: both have an imperative ("take," "leave") followed by three direct objects. In Genesis 22 the stated direct objects (in the Hebrew word order)

---

[1] See also a previously published version by Artur Stele, "The Lord Will Provide: Meditation on Genesis 22," *Dialoque* 30:1 (2018): 18-20.

are: your son, your precious son whom you love, Isaac (here we also have the first occurrence of the word "love" in the Bible); and in Genesis 12 Abraham is commanded to leave three things: your country, your homeland, your father's house. In both cases, each direct object narrows the field more and more until it zeroes in on something or someone unmistakably very dear to the heart of Abraham.

Thirdly, in both places Abraham is given the promise that God will again somehow communicate with him and provide him some additional information regarding the calls. He will either show him or tell him. Genesis 12:1: "'Go . . . to the land that I will show you'" (NRSV); Genesis 22:2: "'. . . upon one of the mountains of which I shall tell you.'"[2]

Here in chapter 22, the promise to have additional communication from God before the actual "goodbye" with his beloved son was a tremendous help to Abraham. The phrase "'. . . on one of the mountains of which I will tell you'" was the assurance he longed for. It was a promise that gave Abraham the much-needed strength to proceed.

These three connections between these two calls also were intended to provide additional help to Abraham to follow God's calling, because they were a reminder of God's leading in the past.

The obvious connection to the first call reminded Abraham "that his obedience to that call had been rewarded with great blessing; now he had the opportunity to show an even greater act of obedience. God was helping him obey by recalling the formal call."[3]

The way that God addresses Abraham in Genesis 22:2 is of great interest.

The divine command *Take* is followed by the particle -nā', which is normally translated something like 'please' or 'I beg you.'. . . -nā', which occurs more than sixty times in

---

[2] Unless otherwise indicated, Scripture quotations are from the New King James Version.

[3] Allen Ross, *Genesis*, Cornerstone Biblical Commentary, Philip W. Comfort, gen. ed. (Carol Stream, IL: Tyndale House, 2008), 141.

Genesis, is used only five times in the entire OT when God speaks to a person. Each timeGod asks the individual to do something staggering, something that defies rational explanation or understanding.[4]

Interestingly enough, out of these five occurrences in the entire Old Testament, in three of them God is addressing Abraham this way—here in Genesis 22:2, and before in Genesis 13:14 and 15:5. Thus, in chapter 22, this unusual way for God to address Abraham serves as a reminder of God's previous communication and leading in Abraham's life. It refers Abraham back to the promises that God has already given to him.

Here we can find a lesson for our own lives. Whenever we go through a difficult place, it is definitely worthwhile to look back and remember God's leading in our past. Ellen G. White so eloquently reminds us of it:

In reviewing our past history, having traveled over every step of advance to our present standing, I can say, Praise God! As I see what the Lord has wrought, I am filled with astonishment, and with confidence in Christ as leader. We have nothing to fear for the future, except as we shall forget the way the Lord has led us, and His teaching in our past history.[5]

In Genesis 12 the call for Abram to leave his country, his homeland, his father's house, was actually an invitation to say "goodbye" to his past; and now in chapter 22 Abraham is invited to say "goodbye" to his future. What is easier to give away—the past, or the future?

Here the principle of substitution is beautifully underscored: Are you willing to give Me your all in exchange for My all to you? You give me your all, and I will give you My all!

Sometimes we can think that God requires too much from us, but it is of great help to see God's requirements always in the light

[4] Victor P. Hamilton, *The Book of Genesis, Chapters 18-50* (Grand Rapids, MI: Eerdmans, 1995), 101.

[5] Ellen G. White, *Life Sketches of Ellen G. White* (Mountain View, CA: Pacific Press, 1915), 196.

of His promises, in the light of what He is giving us in exchange. As we will see from the end of this story, God not only promises us a future above in the kingdom to come, but He blesses us with an abundant life already down here below in the present age.

Abraham's response is presented in a simple but very meaningful expression: "Here I am." He uses this phrase three times in chapter 22. Twice he uses it as a response to God's speaking to him, and once as a response to a question his son Isaac addresses to him. This phrase highlights Abraham's humility on the one hand and his constant readiness to serve on the other.

Genesis 22:2 also names the actual place where Abraham should go, namely, to the "land of Moriah." The only other reference to Moriah is in 2 Chronicles 3:1, where it refers to the Temple hill in Jerusalem. It is a significant piece of information that connects this story with the place where the substitutionary atonement took place through the ultimate sacrifice. Isaac had the privilege of serving as a type that prefigured the actual sacrifice. It is this ultimate substitutionary atonement that made it possible for Abraham to return home together with his beloved son Isaac.

Some have suggested that the etymology of the name Moriah reflects two Hebrew verbs, "Fear" and "See," both of which are of great significance for the entire chapter 22.[6]

Abraham rose early in the morning, split wood for the burnt offering, took his beloved son and two of his young servants, saddled his donkey, and went to the place.

"On the third day Abraham raised his eyes and saw the place from a distance. Abraham said to his young men, 'Stay here with the donkey, and I and the lad will go over there; and we will worship and return to you'" (Gen 22:4-5, NAS95).

"'Stay here with the donkey.'" There is one group that is going up the mountain. In a short while, this group will discover very significant new truth about God and His plan of salvation. The other group will remain where they are, namely, with the donkey.

---

[6] Nahum M. Sarna, *Genesis*, The JPS Torah Commentary (Philadelphia: Jewish Publication Society, 1989), 391.

Abraham describes the purpose of the journey up to the mount with the words, "'we will [go and] worship.'" It is the first time that the word for worship occurs in the Bible. One cannot but think of the importance of worship and the connection it provides to Revelation 14:7.

Abraham also expressed his confidence in God's guidance and earlier promises by stating, "'we will . . . return.'" He is using a plural form here, to include Isaac. This also shows that Abraham understood that God's blessings are not only reserved for the future world to come, but are already a reality here and now. Abraham believed that they would return in a little while, together—he and his beloved son Isaac.

It was this hope that gave him strength to continue the journey, and as verse 6 states, "So the two of them walked on together" (NAS95).

Now as the two walk together, Issac breaks the silence by asking a question that for Abraham was like a knife going through his heart: "My father!" And Abraham responded in the same way he responded earlier to God Himself: "Here I am, my son." Both speakers use the pronoun "my"—"my father," "my son," which underlines the close relationship they enjoyed. The actual question follows: "Behold, the fire and the wood, but where is the lamb for the burnt offering?" (Gen 22:7, NAS95).

Abraham's response is very meaningful. It entails much more than the modern translations can transmit. Usually, Genesis 22:8 is translated: "God will provide for Himself the lamb. . . ." However, one needs to acknowledge that a couple of times in his response Abraham breaks the conventions of Hebrew grammar. He does it not only because he was moved by the question and the whole situation surrounding the unusual call, but first and foremost because he was trying to say more than human language could transmit. Jacques B. Doukhan points to it very appropriately in his new commentary on the book of Genesis by referring to the fact that

the word 'God' is put in the beginning of the sentence before the verbal form. This goes counter to the Hebrew regulation, which normally places the verb before its subject. The intention of this irregularity is to emphasize 'God,' to indicate that the solution is only in God. It is God who will see.[7]

The actual phrase, "God will provide for Himself the lamb," is quite difficult. A more exact translation would be, "God will see in connection to Himself," or, it can be translated, "God will see Himself as the Lamb."[8] In this way, the substitutionary atonement appears even more clearly in the text itself.

This response gave plenty of food for thought to Isaac as they continued to walk together to the place that the Lord showed to Abraham.

Genesis 22: 9-11 says:

Then they came to the place of which God had told him; and Abraham built the altar there and arranged the wood, and bound his son Isaac and laid him on the altar, on top of the wood. Abraham stretched out his hand and took the knife to slay his son. But the angel of the Lord called to him from heaven and said, 'Abraham, Abraham!' And he said, 'Here I am' (NAS95).

"'Abraham, Abraham!'" In Genesis 22:1 God used Abraham's name only once! Here, however, He is calling his name twice, which demonstrates the burning desire of the Lord to share the good news with Abraham on one side, and on the other it demonstrates the willingness of Abraham really to fulfill the order, and the Lord calls out his name twice to stop his sufferings and bring him the "gospel"!

Here we see the heart of God—His desire to share the good news!

Genesis 22:12 quotes God as saying, "'You have not spared your beloved son.'"[9] One cannot help but be reminded of God's ultimate sacrifice to save us, including Isaac himself. See Romans

---

[7] Jacques B. Doukhan, *Genesis*, Seventh-day Adventist International Bible Commentary, v.1 ([Nampa, ID]: Pacific Press & Review and Herald, 2016), 280.

[8] Ibid.

[9] Author's translation.

8:32: "He who did not spare His own Son. . . ." The Septuagint, the Greek translation of the Old Testament (LXX), has the same word in Genesis 22:12 that Paul used in Romans 8:32.

It is also of interest to note that in Genesis 22:12 the actual name "Isaac" is not mentioned, which is another evidence of the typological role he was playing, pointing to the ultimate sacrifice —the Son!

"Then Abraham raised his eyes and looked, and behold, behind him a ram . . ."(Gen 22:13, NAS95). It is of great importance to ask the question, "Why a ram and not a lamb?" After all, Isaac was asking, "Where is the lamb?" Abraham's response was also speaking of a lamb, and yet now, there is a ram? The usage of a ram instead of a lamb connects the story with the day of Atonement. As one commentator indicated, the three words for "burnt offering," "to be seen" in niphal form, and "ram" occur together in the Bible only in Genesis 22, Leviticus 8-9 (the ordination of Aaron and his sons), and Leviticus 16 (the Day of Atonement).[10] In addition, the phrase "raised his eyes and looked, and behold, . . . a ram" finds a parallel in Daniel 8:3: "Then I lifted my eyes and looked, and behold, a ram . . ." (NAS95).

One can truly see the connection of Genesis 22 with the substitutionary atonement of the ultimate sacrifice for all of us.

In verse 14, Abraham then calls the name of the place "YHWH Jireh," usually translated, "The Lord will provide," using the Hebrew verb "ra'ah." This verb means "to see," or "to see [to it]," that is, to provide. At the end of the verse this verb is used again, in the niphal stem, which can be translated as "He will be seen." "In the mount of the Lord He will be seen." He will show Himself, His character, His love! After such a revelation of God's love, it is easy to trust Him, to follow Him, to be guided by Him. Such a God will not let us down; He will provide!

In verse 14, Abraham then calls the name of the place "YHWH Jireh," usually translated, "The Lord will provide," using the Hebrew verb "ra'ah." This verb means "to see," or "to see [to it]," that is, to provide. At the end of the verse this verb is used again, in

---

[10] Hamilton, *Genesis*, 113.

the niphal stem, which can be translated as "He will be seen."[11] "In the mount of the Lord *He will be seen.*" He will show Himself, His character, His love! After such a revelation of God's love, it is easy to trust Him, to follow Him, to be guided by Him. Such a God will not let us down; He will provide!

Genesis 22:23 provides us with additional evidence that God will provide. The genealogy mentions a certain woman's name, the one who will become the future wife of Isaac!

There are two ways. Way one, to stay with the donkey and see nothing special. All the same . . . nothing new . . . always in the company of a donkey.

Or, there is another way. Yes, it is an unknown way, a way that at times even seems to contradict everything you knew and were so sure of, an adventurous way, a way full of surprises, a way to the unknown mountain, a mountain of which He will tell you, a way to the mountain on which He will open to you new light and guidance where you will see His ways, His character, His love, His heart, where you can truly worship Him and finally, finally behold *Him*, see Him and be with *Him* in His place, in the Sanctuary!

The choice is ours:

Behold the Lamb!

Follow the Lamb!

---

[11] Ross, Genesis, 140.

CHAPTER 6

GOING HOME: FACING THE UNEXPECTED

Ángel Manuel Rodríguez

January 28, 1986. The place was the State of Florida. The space shuttle Challenger lifts off to fulfill its mission. The human cargo is seven persons, including a schoolteacher who was the first private citizen to fly on a shuttle. Seventy-three seconds after liftoff, a tragedy occurred. The shuttle exploded, killing the seven astronauts. The question to be answered: Why did this happen? An investigation revealed that the problem was located in two rubber seals on the right side of the rocket booster. It was concluded that the cold weather the day before had damaged the seals. Consequently, there was a leak that resulted in a fire that reached the liquid hydrogen and oxygen, causing an explosion that destroyed the shuttle. As the Challenger broke up, the section where the crew was located separated, but the loss of pressure in the cabin rendered the crew unconscious, and they died for lack of oxygen before the cabin hit the ocean. The people responsible for making sure that the shuttle was ready for the journey did not do what they were expected to do. They should have double checked the seals, but, thinking that everything was fine, they did not do it.

Are we, as leaders, ready for the journey home?

THE EXPERIENCE OF THE LEADER IN THE JOURNEY HOME

Jacob is ready to go home, to the land of his fathers, Abraham and Isaac. He had been in exile for a good many years and is now persuaded that he needs to begin his journey back (Gen 30:25). Realizing that Laban is not willing to let him return home, Jacob decides to leave secretly. The journey home will not be as peaceful as he anticipates. During the journey he will meet three people from his past, and this will prepare him to get home.

Our task is to prepare the world for the coming of the Lord. Are we ready for our journey home?

MEETING ESAU

The first person that Jacob will meet is Esau. He is the enemy from outside, and Jacob does not know how to deal with him. Jacob has a double task: to protect himself from this enemy, and to protect his family. Jacob's brother could make it impossible for him to get home. If he could only resolve this problem, he would be able to reach home and enjoy it.

As a leader, what do you do when you face an outside enemy that is a threat to you and others? Jacob asked the Lord to save him from Esau's hand, but he also developed a strategy. He sent a delegation to explore the territory, to determine the intentions of Esau toward him. He felt he had to know something about the enemy. The report that came back was terrifying. Esau was heading toward him, accompanied by a small army of 400 men. Jacob realized that he would not be able to defeat his enemy.

What can you do to dissuade your enemy from attacking you, from hindering you from going home? Jacob attempts to appease the enemy. The Hebrew word kipper expresses the idea of propitiating Esau (Gen 32:20 [Hebrew, v. 21]). Jacob wanted to make himself acceptable to the enemy in order to avoid the confrontation. He sent gifts to Esau, trying to gain his sympathy and friendship. Here is something that we should learn, once and for all: When heading home, do not try to appease the enemy; do not become his friend. Our enemy is beyond redemption. We should never negotiate with the enemy, because in the process we defeat ourselves. Anyway, what Jacob attempted to do did not work.

The enemy that Jacob was facing came to him from the outside on a mission of destruction. He did not want Jacob to get home. We, too, face an enemy from outside who is superior to us, but not to Jesus. That enemy not only seeks to destroy our spiritual well-being and our loving and trusting fellowship with our Lord; he does not want us to accomplish our responsibilities as leaders who are preparing the world for the coming of the Lord. Perhaps at this very moment some of you are facing this enemy in your fields or institutions, and you do not know how to deal with it. At times, the journey home may appear to be too difficult, and the enemy may seem to be too much for you. But remember what Jesus said: "I have told you these things, so that in me you may have peace. In this world you will have trouble"—leadership is not a trouble-free zone. In fact, leadership is a battlefield! Sometimes we make it a battlefield through our impulsiveness, but in fact it is a place where we face the enemy of God as we attempt to do what the Lord expects us to do. So, Jesus tells us, "'In this world you will have trouble. But take heart! I have overcome the world'" (John 16:33).[1] The victory of Jesus over the enemy assures us that we also will be victorious. But how? He says to us, "I will fight for you."

Surprisingly, Jesus is telling us that since He defeated the enemy for us, we do not have to fight against him. What we have to do is to take hold of Jesus and have peace in the midst of the troubles we confront as we journey home. He defeated the enemy! He broke Satan's power over us. Paul says of Christ, that "having disarmed the powers and authorities, he made a public spectacle of them, triumphing over them by the cross" (Col 2:15). God has done for us what we could not do for ourselves.

God wanted Jacob to get home, and He defeated Esau for Jacob. The text does not say why Esau was not able to attack Jacob, but the book *Patriarchs and Prophets* says that the night before the encounter the Lord came to Esau in a dream and showed him that Jacob was surrounded by the armies of God![2] He was not to touch Jacob, who was God's servant. God sets limits to the attacks of the enemy against those who are marching to Zion. As leaders of God's church, who are daily facing the enemy in our journey home, I will exhort you to remember what Jesus said: "Take heart! I have overcome the world."

MEETING A WARRIOR

The plot of the story suggests that Jacob's problem was not really Esau. Before Jacob met his brother, the enemy, he spent a

---

[1] Unless otherwise indicated, Scripture quotations are from the New International Version.

[2] Ellen G. White, *Patriarchs and Prophets* (Washington, DC: 1890), 198.

night alone, probably praying to the Lord (Gen 32:9-12). It was a difficult night for Jacob, a night of great anguish. He crossed the ford of Jabbok, leaving his family in the land of Canaan, and then crossed back alone. He was outside the promised land with feelings of inadequacy and loneliness. Jacob felt that he was not ready to go home, and this raises the question: Are you ready to go home and to lead others home?

While Jacob was there alone, he suddenly felt a powerful hand taking hold of him. He was shaken to the very bones! The enemy was already there, and he was taken by surprise! He immediately concluded that this was probably Esau or one of his mighty sodiers. They wrestled for a long time. The truth is that at this moment Jacob did not know who his enemy was—but we do. The Stranger wrestling with Jacob was not the enemy, but the Angel of the Lord. Jacob had confused God with the enemy, with the one who would not allow him to go home! Can you imagine that? —confusing the One to whom he prayed for deliverance, the One who had sent a spiritual army of angels to accompany him and his caravan on their journey (Gen 32:1-2), the One who wanted him to reach home and to lead others home, with the enemy! He mistook God for the enemy! What a tragedy! Is it possible for us during our journey to confuse God with the enemy?

Throughout history, humans have considered God to be their enemy. They created temples and performed rituals with the purpose of appeasing or propitiating God. They were afraid of Him. There are today many human beings, even Christians, who believe that God is the enemy. They believe that service to God restricts their freedom, that obedience to His will deprives them of their freedom to eat whatever they want and to use their money and talents in any way they want. They want freedom from a God who appears to them to be oppressive. Consequently, instead of submission to Him, they choose rebellion against His will. They are constantly wrestling with God and His will for their lives, unwilling to submit to Him. They have mistaken God for the enemy.

We find leaders in the Bible who considered the God who appointed them as leaders to be their enemy. They interpreted the divine will for them to be too restrictive, and they decided to go on their own. The prophet Isaiah told the king not to submit to the military coalition formed against him but to trust in the Lord, but he decided to take matters in his own hands. For him, God was the enemy. He did not realize that God's will for us is always good, that what He wants for us is our well-being, that He wants us to be home.

Having said that, I must add that God is described in the Bible as a warrior, even as an enemy (Lam 2:5). But He is the enemy of injustice, oppression, hatred, sin, pride, self-glorification. He hates to see immorality, division, rebellion, envy, and vengeance among His leaders. He is at war against the forces of evil, against Babylon, against those who plan evil against others. He is at war against everything that has damaged His original wonderful creation. He is constantly fighting our enemy, because *our* enemy is *His* enemy. He wants us home.

Yet, God is not my enemy or your enemy, and we should never mistake Him for the enemy. Yes, sometimes He embraces us in what appears to be a wrestling contest, but it is in fact an embrace of love in the middle of our struggles and anguish as leaders.

MEETING JACOB

There they were, wrestling! Two warriors in what Jacob thought was mortal combat; in fact, it was. Jacob was a powerful warrior. Through subterfuge he had defeated his father, Isaac, he had originally defeated Esau, and he had recently defeated Laban. He had always been victorious. And here comes the truth. His imperfections of character made him his own worst enemy. That night God came to fight against Jacob's worst enemy. That night Jacob met Jacob, and he became Israel. We should not dwell on our imperfections, but neither should we forget that we have imperfections, that we also make mistakes as leaders, and that therefore we need to be defeated by the Lord. This is the Jacob who was fully aware of his imperfections and sins. That night, God came to him to liberate Jacob from his worst enemy and therefore to enable him to get home.

What is surprising is that in spite of Jacob's imperfections, sins, and misuse of power, God had not abandoned this man. He had been the constant object of God's kindness and faithfulness, and to him God had made wonderful promises (Gen 32:9-12). God's love is unlimited and abundant toward all of us. He came to

Jacob because of His deep love and concern for him and because God knew that Jacob had tremendous potential as leader of His people.

That night Jacob will die, and Israel will be born! Jacob had to die before reaching home! Jacob's true enemy will be defeated by God. God did not bring anything bad to Jacob; rather, He brought a struggle to free him from himself.

They were wrestling, and Jacob did not know who this Man was until the Man touched Jacob's thigh. This was a gentle touch that defeated Jacob. The pain was deep, and the wrestling was over. This pain was indispensable in order for healing to take place. This is the pain that makes us aware of the fact that we are our own worst enemy, that we need to surrender everything we have to the One who is wrestling with us. Sometimes the Lord has to humiliate us in order to keep us humble, because He has entrusted us with much influence. We need to trust constantly in the Lord in the fulfillment of our responsibilities and walk humbly before Him.

The Angel of the Lord threatened to abandon Jacob to his worst enemy: "Let me go, for it is daybreak. The wrestling is over. You have only one of two choices: surrender or be left alone; begin a new day as a new person or remain what you are." The pain was intense, but knowing now who the enemy was, Jacob decided to hold onto the Lord.

He decided to surrender, to let the old Jacob die. He says to the divine messenger, "Bless me!" His whole life had been a search for that blessing. He bought it from his brother and obtained it by deceiving his father, but he finally realized that God's blessing reaches us through a gift. Surrender has to be for us a daily experience. The Jacob who is inside us must die every day in order for us to be effective leaders. We need God's daily blessing because we cannot buy it. We can only ask for it because it was bought for us through the Son of God, who reconciled us to God.

The divine messenger asked for Jacob's name. Jacob had to be confronted with the person he really was. The Angel seemed to be telling Jacob, "Look at your own character, look at yourself and tell me, what do you see?" This is an important question for us, otherwise we will lose sight of our true sinful nature. Jacob immediately answers: "Oh, My Lord, this is terrible; I see Jacob!"

That night God defeated Jacob. He said to him,

"Jacob, you wrestled with me and you prevailed. My victory over you is your own victory over your worst enemy. When you look at yourself you see Jacob, but I want you to know that when I look at you I see Israel, a person reconciled to God, a new creature. You can now go home and lead others home."

Throughout our lives in our spiritual pilgrimage, we are wrestling with the Lord, and in the process He refines us for the work of leadership. Then He credits us with the benefits of the encounter. We are overcomers; through Him we overcome ourselves.

Then Jacob asked him for his name. The Angel evaded the question with a rhetorical question: "Why do you ask me for my name? I am what you see. There is no duality in me." He seems to be telling Jacob, "I am who I am. To see Me is to know My name, My character." Finally the Angel blessed Jacob. This divine being is the one who can bless us in our journey home. This is divine acceptance! Once God blesses us, no one can take the blessing from us.

CONCLUSION

We are heading home while preparing the world for the coming of the Lord. Yes, the enemy will try to prevent us from reaching home; he will create destruction, chaos, and death on the planet. Nothing is more offensive to him than to see people at peace with God, heading home. He is the enemy, but be courageous, because Christ defeated him.

God also is a warrior. Through the Spirit He is out there fighting against all expressions of evil on this planet. He is not the enemy of the human race but the enemy of every manifestation of the evil that enslaves us. He is the enemy of my enemy but not my enemy, because Christ reconciled me with Him. He is the enemy of our imperfections, and therefore He will embrace us through the Spirit in a struggle against those imperfections.

Then there is my old self, my worst enemy, corrupted by sin. God wants to put the old man to rest, and this must happen before we go home. We are in battle against him, and the way to overcome this enemy is through a daily surrender of all we are to the Lord. His justice is imputed to us, and we are no longer Jacob, but Israel. Have you surrendered the old self to the Lord? Have you said to Him, "My name is Jacob; but please bless me"? His answer will be, "Your name is Israel. Come home!"

CHAPTER 7

THE SURPRISING GOD OF JONAH: TWO LESSONS FOR PASTORS

Jiří Moskala

IMPORTANCE AND STRUCTURE

The Book of Jonah is a jewel in the midst of the Hebrew Bible. It belongs among the 12 Minor Prophets, where it is the fifth one in the sequence. However, Jonah is not a second-league prophet, even though he wrote only 48 verses. His message presents one of the Bible's most significant teachings, one that has immense practical application for pastors. It is momentous that Jonah is the only Old Testament prophet to whom Jesus directly compared Himself (Matt 12:39-41); this indcates that to Jesus Christ the book of Jonah was of utmost importance.

Jonah's story is unique and his message shocking. It not only disrupted the lives of the people of his time, but it also has the power to shake ours. Prophets disturb people's comfort zones and go against their status quo. They blow away people's sinful habits. These servants of God's covenant call people to get rid of all idols and destructive behavior and beseech them to come back to a genuine relationship with God. Their appeals are unambiguous and call for action. One may say that if the message of a prophet docs not lead to repentance, it is not the voice of a true prophet. Jonah, who lived a successful life in the eighth century B.C. (2 Kings 14:25), is not an exception.

His sermon was short, direct, and focused on divine judgment: "Forty more days and Nineveh will be overthrown" (Jonah 3:4).[1]

The theme of the whole book is powerful: "'Salvation comes from the Lord'" (Jonah 2:9), and the book with its four chapters reflects this fundamental truth in its clear literary structure: God saves the sailors (chapter 1), God saves Jonah's physical life (chapter 2), God saves the Ninevites (chapter 3), and finally God saves Jonah spiritually (chapter 4). Jonah's story may be recounted and summarized in the following way: "I will not go" (chapter 1), "I should have gone" (chapter 2), "I will go" (chapter 3), and "I shouldn't have come" (chapter 4). Jonah's heavy presence in the book, however, does not mean that the story is about him, even though he plays a very significant role. This outstanding narrative is ultimately about his God; it is focused on the astonishing God of Jonah.

SURPRISES

It is interesting to observe that the book of Jonah is full of surprises. To name a few: (1) Jonah was the first Hebrew prophet who was sent outside the territory of Israel and Judea to deliver God's message. As a first missionary, he had to go to the momentous city of Nineveh in the domain of the cruel Assyrian enemies of Israel (it was like sending a Jew to Berlin to meet Hitler during the Second World War). (2) The meaning of the name Jonah is "dove." In Nineveh the goddess Ishtar was also symbolized by a dove. This means, then, that the Ninevites had to choose which dove they would follow, their own or the one God sent to them. (3) Jonah was saved in the belly of the big fish. (4) Jonah preached a mini-sermon to the sailors, and they turned to God. (5) The whole city of Nineveh repented. Surprise after surprise!

For me, the biggest surprise in the book of Jonah lies in the fact that everything and everyone obeys God: the storm obeys God; the big fish obeys God; also the wind, plant, worm, and even the sailors and the Ninevites obey God—everyone but the prophet of God. Jonah is the only exception. The Lord's messenger disobeys. Instead of going to the east, he went to the west. The prophet is running away from God! However, it is impossible

---

[1] Unless otherwise indicated, Scripture quotations are from the New International Version.

to escape from God's presence, from His loving and caring omnipresence. We are always accountable to Him.

I repeat: in spite of these facts, the book of Jonah is not primarily about Jonah, but about the God of Jonah. He is a compassionate God, full of grace and mercy. He surprises by His unconditional love. He is the Creator as well as the Redeemer, the Savior. One of the best ways to know the God of Jonah is to study how He treats His disobedient prophet, how He deals with Jonah when he runs away, when he unexpectedly says No to Him.

THE FIRST LESSON: GOD'S BLAZING COMPASSION

In the beginning of chapter 4 of the Book of Jonah, we meet a very angry prophet. The Hebrew text literally says: "It was evil to Jonah, great evil, and he became angry" (4:1). Stunned? One needs to ask what made Jonah so furious. The answer is shocking, because the cause of his rage is God's compassion for the Ninevites! The text is very explicit: "When God saw what they [the Ninevites] did and how they turned from their evil ways, he relented and did not bring on them the destruction he had threatened" (Jonah 3:10). God's prophet is angry because God relents and saves people. Salvation seems evil to Jonah. He would rather die than to see them saved (4:3). Incredible! Unbelievable! In his pride, he is so blind that he wants to see the fulfillment of his prediction rather than the Ninevites' redemption.

Jonah despised these cruel foreigners because of their wickedness and famous cruelty. Astonishingly, Jonah is the first evangelist I know of who had 100% success and was angry because of it. Instead of being joyful and grateful, his frustrations and disappointment with God and His actions sprang up. As humans we have the tendency to push some into heaven, and others we shove out. How comforting to know that God is in charge of each person's salvation!

We can know ourselves better as well as the character of others when something suddenly goes wrong. When we are driving and another driver does an unexpected maneuver, limiting our space, and suddenly we have to jump on our brakes, what we say in this situation and how we react speaks volumes about who we really are, because how we respond in such a situation when our controls are down reveals what is within us. When someone says something against us, makes a mistake, does something wrong, or in a bus or train a person steps on our foot, our looks, gestures, words, and actions speak loudly about our character! The way God reacts to His rebellious prophet is most revealing about His character.

God's reaction to Jonah's rage is full of understanding and patience (another surprising and unexpected feature). The good news in the book is that the God of Jonah does not want to save only the sailors and Ninevites, but also Jonah. He wants to help him experience the true dimensions of conversion and salvation.

PRAYING WHILE ANGRY

It is striking that Jonah prays to God while being angry (4:2). In the past, I thought that this was inappropriate behavior, an unsuitable action. Only later did I understand that this is exactly what God wants from us: to come to Him as we are without a mask, without play-acting or hiding something, but being open and vulnerable (as we see in many of the Psalms). Only when we tell Him everything honestly and sincerely, and we disclose all to Him—even our negative emotions, deep disappointments, and hidden thinking—can He change these things and heal us! According to Psalm 41:4, salvation means healing. If we hide our anger, insults, frustrations, and dissatisfactions inside us, these negative feelings will grow, choke us, take the joy out of life, and eventually kill our spiritual life. When Jonah prays to God, there is hope for Jonah. When we pray, there is hope for us.

Jonah had good information about God, but unfortunately, this "head religion" did not make him a kind, warm, loving, and sensitive person. He knew that His God was "'a gracious and compassionate God, slow to anger and abounding in love, a God who relents from sending calamity'" (4:2; he quotes God Himself —see Exod 34:6-7), but no ethical consequences of this fact appeared in his life. He displays no sign of God's gracious compassion. His behavior reveals bad morality because his heart was not changed by this knowledge. An intellectual religion is not enough. Such a religion becomes a philosophy. If one's life reveals a cold heart and damaging attitudes, it means that the trans-forming grace of God has not yet been fully accepted, because

God's amazing grace is always a transforming grace. God's love warms the people around us.

Jonah was tired and disappointed that after he had gone throughout Nineveh for forty days announcing God's judgment upon the city, the destruction had not yet occurred. This unbalanced him. He states, "'Now, LORD, take away my life, for it is better for me to die than to live'" (Jonah 4:3). If God is as good as Jonah claims his God is, the God of compassion, grace, patience, and abounding love, then it should be a great pleasure to live with such a beautiful God. But no, Jonah wishes for his own death. He is disappointed with this compassionate God and has become bitter. It would be better to be dead, he claims. He is embarrassed that his preaching regarding God's judgment had not resulted in the city's destruction, so he is dejected.

We read in the biblical account how the Lord peacefully reacted: "'Is it right for you to be angry?'" (Jonah 4:4). At this point, Jonah does not want any further discussion of the matter with the Lord. Hurt and insulted, he goes out of the city to the east (from the east God comes—see Ezek 43:1-2, 4; cf. Isa 24:15; Rev 16:12) and made for himself a shelter to see what would occur. From there he was waiting for God's fire from heaven to burn the city or for an earthquake to bury them. "There he made himself a shelter, sat in its shade and waited to see what would happen to the city" (Jonah 4:5b).

Once again, the Lord intervenes in favor of Jonah, because He wants to help him to understand and grow. God wants to save him from his anger, prejudice, hatred, enmity, racism, exclusivism, self-centeredness, and feelings of superiority. The Lord made a plant to grow for Jonah to provide shade for him: "Now the LORD God appointed a plant and made it come up over Jonah, that it might be a shade over his head, to save him from his discomfort" (Jonah 4:6, ESV).

For the first time in the book, we read that Jonah is happy, he is "extremely happy" (4:6b, NASB 1995). The cause of his happiness was a thing, a plant, which consequently became his comfort. He is not rejoicing over the people and their repentance, but over the pleasant shade. Jonah is "dancing" for joy around the plant, because it provided shade for him. Finally, Jonah is happy!

What is the source of your happiness? Possessions? People? Salvation? External happiness is only temporal. The most important thing is not what we have, but who we are: saved and wishing salvation for others. God teaches Jonah this simple yet crucial lesson. God intervenes once more: "But at dawn the next day God provided a worm, which chewed the plant so that it withered" (Jonah 4:7). Thus, by the following day, the enjoyable plant was dead. The cause of his external happiness was gone, and Jonah pities his loss and himself: "'It is better for me to die than to live'" (Jonah 4:8c, ESV).

Jonah is crying over a plant but wishes the death of many people! What a paradox! It is like some commanders during war who order the execution of thousand without mercy, but when they see that their beloved dog or a fish in their aquarium is dead, they cry over it—pitying animals but killing people without any sympathy!

The biblical text points out that now God again questions Jonah but specifically about the plant, and it reveals Jonah's quick, angry answer: "But God said to Jonah, 'Is it right for you to be angry about the plant?' 'It is,' he said. 'And I'm so angry I wish I were dead'" (Jonah 4:9). God asks Jonah to pause and think, because it is not at all right to be so upset because of the plant that he had neither planted nor worked for.

Then come the two last verses of the book, the culmination point, when God approaches Jonah with the final question. But what a question! The Lord declares:

"'You have been concerned about this plant, though you did not tend it or make it grow. It sprang up overnight and died overnight. And should I not have concern for the great city of Nineveh, in which there are more than a hundred and twenty thousand people who cannot tell their right hand from their left—and also many animals?'"

(Jonah 4:10). To paraphrase these verses, the Lord says to him:

Jonah, you have pitied the plant, but I have pitied people. You have cried over a thing, but I have showed compassion for persons. Instead of lamenting over a plant, which appeared without any of your own effort, work, or achievement, should you not be concerned for people and have compassion for them? Should you not do the same as I did?

There is no recorded answer from Jonah to this divine question. If Jonah is the author of the book, as I assume, then the answer is clear. He records his experience to warn his readers not to fall into the same abyss of hardness of heart, but instead to be open to people who are different from us, who may think, feel, and act differently than we do, as God has the power to accept and change these people.

God's compassion is incomprehensible, incomparable, astonishing, challenging, and transforming! The Book of Jonah confronts us with the real issues of life. God wants us to have courage to face the challenges of life with a proper attitude. He desires us to put down all barriers of religion, race, color, education, geography, language, gender, and politics. Without reservation, He wants to save everyone. The warm compassion of God for people is contrasted with the cold attitude of the prophet. Jonah confesses that he had an attitude of ice toward others and challenges us not to commit the same mistake he did. Jonah was commissioned but not committed.

THE SECOND LESSON: DIFFERENT KINDS OF OBEDIENCE

Let us consider the life of Jonah once again but from a different perspective. God as a Sovereign Lord calls Jonah to go to Nineveh to deliver an important message of judgment—get up, go, and preach (Jonah 1:1-2). He refuses, disobeying God's commands, and the result is that the prophet "goes down." The biblical text stresses his downward movement while he runs away from God. First, he went down to Joppa, then to the harbor, after that down to the boat, then to the lowest place in the boat, and finally we encounter him at the bottom of the ocean. The downward movement is very graphic. Every time we run from God, we go down!

Then he cried to the Lord, and the compassionate, gracious, and loving God saved him. Jonah praised the Lord for his deliverance when he was still in the belly of the big fish (see Jonah 2). Even though he accepted salvation personally, he took it selfishly.

It is true that we need to take salvation personally (Jesus Christ died for me!), but it is tragic when we take it narrow-mindedly: salvation for me, yes, for my family, friends, group, tribe, nation, but not so much for others. We always have the tendency to dictate to God whom to save and whom to assign to perdition. It is so refreshing to know that we have no power to preclude the salvation of others and that God ultimately decides this matter because He understands human hearts and minds.

Afterwards God called Jonah for the second time. "Get up, go to Nineveh and preach!" (see Jonah 3:1-2). Jonah got up, went to Nineveh, and preached. His behavior leads to a crucial question: Was he now an obedient prophet? Well, he preached to the Ninevites, but what was his attitude toward them? He proclaimed the Word of God, but in his heart was hatred, enmity, anger, bitterness, and prejudices! He experienced God's grace but was not willing to extend this same grace to others. He still needed to experience a true conversion.

These exegetical observations lead us to a very significant conclusion: God does not want our obedience. Let me finish this scandalous statement: God does not want our obedience to be of Jonah's type. This kind of obedience is only for appearance—on the surface, outward, and shallow. God does not want us to obey Him like trained horses or dogs, or like parrots, where we only repeat after Him what He said without allowing Him to transform us by His Word, grace, and Spirit. Nor does He want our obedience to be like the obedience of soldiers who follow commands without thinking or understanding, something like the Nazi officers claimed during the Nuremberg International War Tribunal in Germany after the Second World War: "We did nothing wrong; we only obeyed orders." Obedience means responsibility!

God, of course, wants us to obey Him but desires that our obedience come as a result of knowing Him for who He is (through His words and experience). He desires that our obedience spring from our heart and be motivated by gratitude, thankfulness, and love for Him and His incomprehensible goodness. When we are attracted to the kindness of God (Rom 2:4), then we do not follow Him because we have to, but because we want to. Our Lord really longs to see us behaving as responsible sons and daughters of God!

Obedience is not a mere outward compliance but a service of love. Superficial obedience is not enough! True, genuine obedience is never forced or blind. It comes out of the practical knowledge of and relationship with the true, loving, and holy God. This obedience does not mean that we will always understand God's purposes, providence, and events in our lives, but that we will follow Him no matter what, because we personally know Him and His love for us. Only in this way can we indeed be loving, warm, contagious, and compassionate people who show Adventism in a godly and attractive way.

So, what?

The book of Jonah is open ended. Why does the book end with a question mark? Because it calls for a reaction. We are now an integral part of the story. The response is hanging in the air and waiting for us to answer. Only the reader—meaning you and I—can answer God's pertinent and ultimate question. The Lord is asking: What is your attitude toward those people who are different from you, people of different color, gender, education, position, nationality, religion,ethnicity, or behavior, and who according to our prejudices do not deserve God's mercy? Do we have the same unselfish and warming love in our hearts toward other people as our unselfish God has? Do we have the same compassion toward them as God demonstrates?

Jonah encourages us not to be as cold to others as he was toward the Ninevites. Can we react differently and actually warm their hearts in order for them to be attracted to our God of love, truth, justice, and freedom?

God comes and asks all of us individually through Jonah's story to answer for ourselves: What type of obedience is shown in my submission to God? Is my obedience superficial, forced, and automatic, or coming from the heart, from a deep knowledge of God's goodness? Is it out of love and gratitude and as a sign that I have accepted my responsibility as God's child? God waits for you and me to answer without delay, correctly, and with enthusiasm. God wants to send to the world messengers who are saved by God's grace and transformed by His Spirit's power so that they can be His instruments for the salvation of many. Are you willing to work closely with Him and go forward without making excuses? Are you willing to witness to people around you and make disciples for Jesus of those who are willing and ready to follow Him?

CHAPTER 8

IS THERE BREAD IN THE HOUSE OF BREAD?

Artur A. Stele

The postmodern times in which we are living today are best compared with the time of the Judges in the Old Testament. The main characteristic of the time of the Judges is well presented in the Book of Judges itself:

"In those days there was no king in Israel; everyone did what was right in his own eyes" (Judg 21:25).[1]

The story of the Book of Ruth took place at that very time: "Now it came about in the days when judges governed, that there was a famine in the land. And a certain man of Bethlehem in Judah went to sojourn in the land of Moab with his wife and his two sons" (Ruth 1:1).

Then the following text explicitly gives the name of this man who went to sojourn: "The name of the man was Elimelech" (Ruth 1:2).

It is interesting to note that the story took place at the time when there was no king in Israel, and yet the Book of Ruth makes a special effort to explicitly mention the name of the man: Elimelech!

The meaning of the name actually is: "My God is King!" Although there was no king in Israel, no visible king, the name of Elimelech pointed to an unseen reality, namely, that there was and still is a King above, a King of the universe! At times, we all go through circumstances in life when it seems that we are left alone, with no one here to help or even understand us. But there

---

[1] Scripture quotations are taken from the New American Standard Bible, 1995 edition.

is a different reality. There is the One who is unseen, but who is real, and He is in control!

The book of Ruth provides a window through which we can see the providences of God at work. However, one must agree with words attributed to John Flavel, who stated that "The providences of God . . . are like Hebrew words: they can only be read properly backwards."[2]

When going through difficulties, we usually see things only from our own perspective; however, the Book of Ruth opens a small window for us that enables us to see things from God's perspective.

Elimelech and his family were living in Bethlehem.

The name Bethlehem actually means "House of Bread."

What a tragedy—in the "House of Bread," there was *no bread*!?

And as a result, the people were forced to leave the House of Bread in a search of a place that had bread.

In this search for bread, Elimelech and his family went to Moab.
The Book of Deuteronomy actually states that this was exactly the place that did not receive the people of Israel with bread:

"'No. . . Moabite . . . shall ever enter the assembly of the Lord, because they did not meet you with food and water on the way when you came out of Egypt" (Deut 23:3-4).

Where the word "food" appears in this passage, the Hebrew actually uses the word "bread"!

"'Because they did not meet you with bread'"!

The physical famine and hunger described in the Book of Ruth also marked a time of spiritual famine in Bethlehem, as well as throughout Israel.

The first book of Samuel (1 Sam 3:1) provides one of the best descriptions of the spiritual hunger in the time of Judges. The description also fits well in our time today: "Now the boy Samuel

---

[2] https://gracequotes.org/author-quote/john-flavel/ (accessed October 14, 2021).

was ministering to the Lord before Eli. And word from the Lord was rare in those days, visions were infrequent."

Could it be that also today in the House of Bread, there is *no* bread?!

Could it be that today, from the pulpits in our churches, people are not getting the spiritual bread they need?

Is it possible that our people today are forced to leave the House of Bread in a search for bread?

Is it possible that we are forcing our people out to go to the land of Moab where there is no real bread?

Is it possible that today many church members are not attending the worship on Sabbath but rather are searching in the Internet valleys of Moab for spiritual food?

Have you heard a cry from church members: "Pastor, we are hungry for the Word of God"?

Research shows convincingly that one of the main reasons why people of all ages are leaving the church today is that they are not getting biblical messages that are relevant to their everyday needs. And so, the big question remains: "Is there bread in the house of bread?"

I will never forget my first trip to Moldova after being elected as Euro-Asia Division president. It was a time when Moldova was experiencing very difficult economic challenges. The Seventh-day Adventist Church was celebrating 110 years in that country. On Sabbath, many thousands of believers all across the country were gathered in the best hall in Kishinev. Many guests and government officials were present. According to the program, I was to speak after a representative of the Parliament spoke.

The speech of the Parliament representative was an unforgettable one. He shared a letter that a small boy wrote to God and mailed through the regular postal system. The boy was growing up in a home where a single mother had to care for several children. The children often asked mom where their father was. The mother told them that they do not have a father here on earth, but they do have a heavenly father. So, the oldest boy, around

7 or 8 years old, decided to write a letter to his heavenly father, in which he asked him to send them 100 leys (the local currency in Moldova). The boy put the letter in the envelope, and besides writing his own address, he wrote with big letters: "TO GOD."

When the envelope arrived at the main post office, no one knew how to send the letter to God. Someone finally suggested, "Let's send the letter to the Parliament. They have nothing to do anyway, so let them figure out how to send this letter to God." When the envelope was delivered to the Parliament speaker, he called the chairmen of different committees together and presented them the challenge. He opened the envelope and read the letter, asking at the end: "What should we do?" One representative responded: "Let's not disappoint the small boy. Let's put at least 10 ley in an envelope and send it to the boy." This suggestion found support, and they mailed 10 leys to the boy in a special Parliament envelope.

Several weeks went by, and a new letter from the same boy arrived for the speaker of the Parliament. He called the chairs of different committees together again and opened and read the letter, in which the boy wrote to God:

"My dear heavenly Father! Thank you so much for caring about our family, and thank you for the money, but please, next time, when you decide again to help us, do not send the money via the Parliament, because they kept 90 leys for themselves and sent me only 10."

I ask myself while I am preaching—how much bread are we delivering to our listeners? Can it be that we, as God's channels of blessings, are not providing the real bread, but only some crumbs from it?

Might it even be that we ourselves don't have the bread? You cannot share what you don't have.

Naomi and Ruth made a decision to return to Bethlehem—the House of Bread—after they heard that the Lord had visited His people in giving them bread! Only when it became known that the bread was back again in the House of Bread did the remnant of Elimelech's family decide to return to the House of Bread.

"Then she arose with her daughters-in-law that she might return from the land of Moab, for she had heard in the land of Moab that the LORD had visited His people in giving them food" (Ruth 1:6). Again, the Hebrew word for "bread" is used here!

And they returned back to Bethlehem "at the beginning of barley harvest" (Ruth 1:22).

Throughout the history of Christianity, beginning from the times of Jesus (Mark 2:1-2), the churches were well attended, and reformation took place only when the Living Bread, the Living Word of God, was abundantly available from the pulpits.

Interestingly, before Naomi and Ruth decided to return back to Bethlehem, Naomi had begged her daughters-in-law to turn back and stay in Moab (Ruth 1:7-15). It reminds us of the reaction of the priest Eli, as a number of times he sent Samuel back to sleep, not recognizing that God was calling him (1 Sam 3:5-6, 8).

In urging her daughters-in-law to go back, Naomi did not realize that she was actually sending away her future, her provider, her hope, her "bread."

Orpah decided to follow the advice of her mother-in-law, and she turned back. However, Ruth said:

> Do not urge me to leave you or turn back from following you; for where you go, I will go, and where you lodge, I will lodge. Your people shall be my people, and your God, my God. Where you die, I will die, and there I will be buried. Thus may the LORD do to me, and worse, if anything but death parts you and me (Ruth 1:16-17).

So, both of them went on to Bethlehem.

The second chapter of the Book of Ruth presents the developing story of the life of the two women in Bethlehem. At first, it seems that good things happen by chance (Ruth 2:3). However, looking at the story from the end rather than from the beginning, the reader realizes the beauty of God's plans and His providences.

As we turn to the last recorded words of Ruth in the Book of Ruth, we start seeing a glimpse of light coming through a window of God's providences. "She said, 'These six measures of barley he gave to me, for he said, "Do not go to your mother-in-law empty-handed"'" (Ruth 3:17).

The last phrase is quite significant: "Do not go to your mother-in-law empty-handed." This phrase reminds the readers of the statement Naomi made to the people of Bethlehem when she returned to the city. "'Do not call me Naomi; call me Mara, for the Almighty has dealt very bitterly with me. I went out full, and the LORD has brought me back empty. Why do you call me Naomi, since the LORD has witnessed against me and the Almighty has afflicted me?'" (Ruth 1:20-21).

Naomi had stated, "I went out full, and the LORD has brought me back empty." Now the last recorded words of Ruth in the book are actually the words of Boaz: "Do not go to your mother-in-law empty-handed."

Ruth went out empty, but now she is returning fully loaded with barley, with bread! What is significant here is that the barley was not just for Ruth but was actually for Naomi also.

From a human perspective Naomi sees herself as empty-handed—not blessed, but rather cursed by God. But looking through the window of God's providences, we can see that God has not only satisfied Naomi's hunger, but He has given her much more —a family tree, and what a tree it was!

Through the providences of God, Naomi will become the grandmother of David, who will be anointed as a king of Israel in Bethlehem, the House of Bread! But if one keeps looking father into the future through the window of God's providences, one will see that Naomi will become not only the grandmother of David, the king of Israel, but she will become the great-great- (etc.)-grandmother of Jesus who will be born in Bethlehem —the King of the universe, the One who will one day say, "I am the Bread of Life!"—the One who will one day say, "I am the resurrection and the life!"

He is the One who will one day resurrect Naomi's husband and return her two sons.

Naomi, don't look at your empty hands now. Don't forget the meaning of your husband's name: "My God is King." He will have the last word in your life!

Keep looking up for the window through which you will see some glimpses of God's providences! You will see the One who is able to turn a curse into a blessing, a sorrow into a joy, a hopeless situation into a new beginning!

> Then the women said to Naomi, 'Blessed is the Lord who has not left you without a redeemer today, and may his name become famous in Israel. May he also be to you a restorer of life and a sustainer of your old age; for your daughter-in-law, who loves you and is better to you than seven sons, has given birth to him.' Then Naomi took the child and laid him in her lap, and became his nurse (Ruth 4:14-16).

The response of Naomi to the last recorded words of Ruth is quite significant as well. It actually also represents the last recorded words of Naomi to Ruth in the Book of Ruth: "Then she said, 'Wait my daughter, until you know how the matter turns out; for the man will not rest until he has settled it today'" (Ruth 3:18).

For the word "wait," the Hebrew Bible actually uses a word that is better translated as "sit down."

"'Sit down, my daughter . . . for the man will not rest until he has settled it today.'" Who is this man? It is Boaz, who in the same chapter is presented several times as a kinsman, a *goel*, a redeemer!

The redeemer will not rest—will not be quiet, will not relax, will not be inactive. He will continue working behind the scenes. It is because he will be working that you can sit down and relax!

What a wonderful message to all of us! Our redeemer, who is the King of the universe, is constantly working behind the scenes—not against us, but for us! I can rest, because He will not rest until He has settled it!

Note that in the beginning of the Book of Ruth, we find two women, Orpah and Ruth, who have to make a difficult decision.

One makes the decision to give up and return home. After she makes this decision, she disappears from the history. Her name is never mentioned again in the Book of Ruth. The second woman makes the decision not to give up the One to whom the name of her father-in-law was pointing. She decides to go with Naomi and serve her and the King of the universe. She makes the right decision, and her name not only keeps being mentioned in the Book of Ruth, but her name comes up in the genealogy not only of David the king, but actually of the One who is the real *Goel*—Jesus Christ! Ruth does not disappear from history; she in fact *makes* history!

At the end of the Book of Ruth, there are two men who have to make a decision: Both have the right to be kinsman, the redeemer, the *goel*. The one who was actually the closest relative decides not to get involved, and he is the only specific person to appear in the whole Book of Ruth whose name is not mentioned at all. At best he is mentioned with a Hebrew expression that means "a certain one," or "so and so." The other man, Boaz, decides to get involved, to help, and thus becomes not only the key figure of the whole book, but what is even more important, he becomes the grandfather of the king and also a figure who symbolizes the great King and the true *Goel*!

What role are you planning to play in these times when there is little or no bread in the House of Bread?

The story of the Book of Ruth takes place when there was no king in Israel.

The book starts with a sad statement that there was no bread in the House of Bread, but it finishes with plenty of bread in the House of Bread!

It finishes with a family tree that will lead to the One who later will say, "I am the Bread of Life!" (see John 6:48).

It finishes with pointing our attention to the One who is the King of kings, who always was, is, and will be the King of kings.

This why there is a special mention of the name Elimelech (My God is King), even during a time when there was no king in Israel.

He, our true *Goel*, will not rest till the matter of providing Bread for His children will be settled.

He will not rest till Bread is provided to a secular and postmodern world as well!

Today, the choice is ours: Will we get involved in providing Bread to the House of Bread? Will we get involved in providing hope where hope is lacking, in pointing the attention of the people to the window of God's providences, in pointing to the Redeemer who is not relaxing, who is not resting, who is not sitting till the matter is solved?

Is there Bread in the House of Bread?!

CHAPTER 9

IS ALL WELL?

Ángel Manuel Rodríguez

All seemed to be back to normal. Naaman had left, physically and spiritually healed. He came in darkness, lacking the knowledge of the true God, and left as a member of the people of Israel. He would be God's ambassador in Syria. Elisha was grateful to the Lord for what He did for Naaman—healing him in a miraculous way from his leprosy. His God does not discriminate against any people; His offer of salvation is available to all, be they women, men, children, old or young. He does not know about ethnic or national boundaries. He is merciful to all. Elisha was proud of his wonderful God, the God of Israel. This was a happy ending to a story of fear, uncertainty, and pride. Yet, there is another chapter, a new plot that will be developed in three different scenes. One takes place in the mind or heart of a person, another on a dusty road, and the third one in the house of the prophet.

THE POWER OF SHALOM

FIRST SCENE: WHAT IS IN THE HEART?

As the new plot begins to develop, the person of Gehazi is introduced to us. He was alone with his thoughts, speaking to himself. The biblical narrator allows us to listen to the inner reflections of Gehazi. As we listen, we aresurprised by what we hear. He was thinking about Naaman, Elisha, and himself. He was analyzing what took place a moment ago; he was thinking about the healing of Naaman. This is a common human trait —we think about what happened to us and to those around us, and sometimes we have second thoughts about the decisions made. If we could only go back and change the decisions made! But the past is unalterable. Or so it seems. Gehazi had concluded that it was not too late, that since the events were still evolving, he might be able to rewrite the ending of the story. What he seemed to have ignored was that from the divine perspective the story of Naaman had ended. In any case, Gehazi decided to add a new chapter to the story in order to alter its ending. And he was successful!

Let us listen to his inner thoughts, because perhaps we may be able to find there our own thoughts. By listening to them we will come to know this man a little better, and possibly ourselves. too. He was thinking about the prophet Elisha, evaluating how he had dealt with Naaman. He concluded that the prophet had acted foolishly in rejecting the gifts that Naaman offered him. According to Gehazi, the gift of the Spirit was power, a power that could be used to enrich us and to provide a better life for us on earth. But the prophet did not take advantage of the situation. He was a fool. Gehazi had a low opinion of the man of God, his master, and had a judgmental attitude. He also had an opinion about Naaman—he considered him unworthy of human sympathy and respect. He disrespectfully referred to him as "this Naaman, the Aramean."[1] He was not an Israelite but an enemy of Israel who had killed many Israelites and taken others as prisoners of war. According to Gehazi, Elisha should have taken advantage of him. After all, his wealth was partially taken from the Israelites. Gehazi had good reason to dislike and even hate this man! In his heart there was a significant amount of ethnic and national prejudice against Naaman. Naaman was his enemy, and if he could take some of his wealth, why should not he do it? By criticizing Elisha's behavior and emphasizing Naaman's ethnicity or nationality, he felt justified in what he was about to do.

Gehazi persuaded himself that it was correct to go and get some of the money Naaman brought with him. He had no respect for the prophet of God and for what God had done for a non-Israelite. In fact, he had no respect for God. But underlying all of that was something that he never mentioned in his thoughts—namely, his selfishness. He was not interested in serving others but in self-service. Elisha saw his ministry as one of serving others, bringing to them the light of the knowledge

---

[1] Scripture quotations are from the New American Standard Bible, 1995 edition.

of the true God, but that was not his servant's view. According to Gehazi, people were there to make his life better, for him to be enriched by them. He wanted to provide for his future in order to enjoy a good life now. This was his real problem, but it was too painful for him to recognize it. He had forgotten that the Spirit comes to our lives to transform us and notto satisfy our desire for power or to nurture our greed. He would rather justify his decision on some other basis in order to feel comfortable with the decision that he was about to make. We call this self-deception. He introduced his decision with a religious oath! "'As the LORD lives, I will run after him and take something from him.'" This man, full of greed, prejudice, and with a judgmental attitude against God's prophet, decided in the name of the Lord that he would go and get some of the wealth of Naaman.

He was the servant of Elisha! They dwelt together and traveled together. He ministered to the man of God and occasionally counseled him about what to do. Coming into contact with true servants of God is a wonderful thing, but such a casual contact does not make us holy. Judas was very close to Jesus, but he never became like Jesus. On the contrary, he stood for the very things Jesus opposed. Yes, being among the saints is good, but we need more than that. We need to appropriate that holiness; we need to let God be in charge of our story and to guide the narrative of our lives.

SECOND SCENE: IS ALL WELL?

Our thoughts are capsules of energy that determine our behavior. Gehazi decided to run after Naaman, and the Bible says, "So Gehazi pursued [*rādaph*, "chase," "hunt"] Naaman." For Gehazi, Naaman was the game in the hunt. He was no longer a human being. Our respect for others is determined by our respect for God. Gehazi set a goal for his life, and he hit the road in order to achieve it. Life is a journey. We live on the road, pursuing something, and what we pursue reveals who we are and our concerns and fears. What are you running after? As we run, occasionally we have to hear the question, "Is all well with you?" Gehazi had to run because Naaman was already traveling ahead of him.

The two men were to meet again. The first time they met, Gehazi had a message for him from the prophet—Go and wash yourself in the Jordan—and it was logical for Naaman to conclude that now he may have another message from the prophet for him. So he stopped the caravan. These were two quite different men. They form a picture; one was the negative and the other the positive. The first voice we hear in this scene is that of Naaman: "'Is all well?'" What a question! It must have hit Gehazi hard. In the Hebrew we have only one word, *Hashalom?* "Is there peace?" The term *shalom* includes the idea of integrity, wholeness, health, well-being; it refers to a life that is in order. It is a very rich term. The question was, "Are you, Gehazi, at peace, in complete harmony with your inner being, with others and with God? Tell me, Gehazi, is all well with you?"

This was the last chance Gehazi had to reconsider what he was about to do. He could have said, "No, my lord, there is no peace with me. There is something deeply wrong with my life. I must go back to my master because only the prophet can heal me and make me whole."

Let me ask you today, Is all well with you? Sin is very deceitful and makes us believe that "all is well," when in reality, not all is well. A life at peace is a life that is integrated around a center it has a nucleus that orients it and makes it whole.

Gehazi persuaded himself that what he was doing was right. He had a quick answer for Naaman: "'All is well.'" (*Shalom!*). This was the first lie in a list of lies Gehazi uttered. Evil has to be covered up, and the only way to do it is to cover it up with misinformation, with deceit. He was not at peace with God or with any other person. Peace is a gift of God and is granted to us through the Prince of Peace. We have peace only when we have Him in our lives, when His values become our values, when we live a life of service to others as He did, and when we constantly rely on His forgiving grace.

Naaman was at peace with God, and he provided for us a profile of a person at peace. He was at peace because he had given his life to the God of Israel. He was the object of divine healing; God made him whole physically and spiritually. He was a new man in the Lord. He met the Prince of Peace in the waters of the Jordan. To the question, "Naaman, is all well with you?" He would have shouted with joy, "All is well with me! I was sick, but now I am healed!" And it showed in his demeanor.

The person who can say "Yes, all is well with me," is one who is *humble*, who does not pretend to be more than he or she is. The proud Naaman was now the humble Naaman who was willing to descend from his chariot to talk to the servant of the prophet. A few hours before, when he went to the house of the prophet, he stood in front of the house on his chariot. The proud minister of defense of Syria was now a humble servant of God. All was well with him because he *respected* others. There was no prejudice in his heart against this Israelite. For him, all humans were valuable. It was prejudice that had led him to attack the Israelites living along the border with Syria. That prejudice was gone, because now he was also part of the people of God. Among those who are well, nationality, ethnicity, and gender distinctions are no longer important. Prejudice is expelled from the human heart through the love of God. Every human being is respected and treated as equal. We often hear that respect is something you earn; but this is wrong. In our dealings with others respect is a given because they, like us, are children of God.

"Naaman, is all well with you?" In the heart of a person who can say, "All is well with me," there is a natural disposition to *serve* others. Selfishness does not rule such a life. When Gehazi lied for a second time, Naaman showed great benevolence and gave him more than he requested. What Naaman suspected appears to be true; Gehazi claimed to have a message from the prophet for him: "Two students came and they need clothing and some money. Would it be possible to get from you two changes of clothes and a talent of silver?" Naaman offered two talents of silver and pressured Gehazi to take them. He gave of what he had because he had given his life to God, to be used as He pleased. This unselfishness is possible when all is well with you. "Is all well with you?" Or is something disrupting your inner being, damaging your wholeness?

Finally, all was well with Naaman, and it showed by his revealing a spirit of *compassion* to others. A talent of silver weighed about 75 pounds. It was difficult for one person to carry it. Now, Gehazi had to carry two talents of silver—150 pounds. Naaman knew that this was too much for Gehazi, and he ordered two of his soldiers to carry the loads for Gehazi. "This Aramean," as Gehazi had referred to him, was kind to him and was concerned about his well-being. He wanted to preserve the *shalom* of Gehazi; a *shalom* that was not there. Naaman was at peace with God, journeying on God's road, and that peace was visible. "Is all well with you?"

Gehazi began his journey back, wondering what he was going to do with the two servants of Naaman. He did not plan for this detail, and he certainly did not want to be seen with them. He had to come up with a plan to get rid of them. There was no peace in his heart. He had to hide his sin, which had now taken a concrete form. It was no longer hidden in his heart; it was visible. He knew what to do! He would dismiss them before they got to the city. Now he carried the load of his sin and realized that it was indeed heavy.

THIRD SCENE: WHERE HAVE YOU BEEN?

Gehazi went back home, but everything had changed. From now on, he could only pretend to be the same. He had a split personality, or multiple personalities; one showed up when he was in the presence of the prophet, and the other when he was away from him. He was not integrated around one center. Not all was well with him. He was aware of the fact that he had done something wrong, because he lied and he hid the goods. Yes, he could only pretend to be the same and behave like the servant of Elisha. But he now had a secret. I imagine the prophet asking him in a rather casual way, "I missed you, Gehazi; where have you been?" He lies again, "'Your servant went nowhere [*'āneh we'ānāh*]'" ("I was neither here nor there"). Was he really lying? The truth is that he had gone "nowhere." Our journey in life has a destination only when we travel on the way of the Lord. Otherwise, we are going nowhere! That is the land of death, the land of deceitfulness, the place where we have no deep respect for others, not even for God's will for us. Gehazi had visited the place of greed and was about to discover that such a place led nowhere. Of course, that was not what he had in mind when he said, "'Your servant went nowhere.'"

From that point on, Gehazi was silent—the silence of someone who is proven to be guilty. The prophet told him something that he should have known. He told him that when he left the house, he was not traveling alone, that he had a silent companion and a witness; the Lord was traveling with him. He ran, and the Lord ran with him; he walked back, and the Lord walked back with him. God travels on the road we travel, and that makes a difference. We never travel alone! He was traveling with Naaman, and "all was well" with him. He was at peacewith God. He traveled with Gehazi in order to make him know that not all was well with him. He gave him a last chance to repent, because He was traveling with him. When he was asked, "Is all well with you?" he should have said, "No, all is not well with me!" "Is all well with you?" The prophet tells his servant that the silent companion showed him what had taken place.

The moment of truth has arrived. The unveiling of the deepest secret in Gehazi's heart was now to take place. Elisha told him,

> I know what you were thinking. You were thinking about your future and the need for you to take charge of it. You feared facing troubles and difficulties, and you tried to find a way to avoid them. You were thinking about getting enough financial resources to buy a piece of land, to plant a vineyard, to buy animals, tohave servants and clothing. You wanted a good future, and you concluded that the way to do it was by taking some of the gifts of Naaman instead of waiting on the Lord. You said in your heart, 'I will run after him and take something from him.' I want you to know that your wish has been granted to you. The Lord, not Naaman, is going to share with you the only thing He took from Naaman—his leprosy.

> I ask you again, "Is all well with you?"

The prophet seemed to be telling Gehazi, there was nothing wrong about planning for the future, but this was neither the time nor the way to do it. We are to trust in the love and care of the Lord in order to honor God in all we do. What was the problem? Did not Naaman have more than he needed? Was he not willing to share it with them? Why the severity of the judgment? Placing the story in the context of the healing practices of the ancient Near East may help us to understand the narrative.

In Mesopotamia and Syria, a distinction was made between the physician, who diagnosed diseases, and what we today would call the pharmacist. A sick person could throw himself or herself at the mercy of the gods, go to the physician to get a prescription, or visit the pharmacist to get medication. Very often the physician was a temple official and consequently did not charge for his services. The pharmacist charged for services rendered. Elisha was not a physician—he did not work in the temple—but neither was he a pharmacist, who charged for his services. He was a prophet of the Lord, and it was the Lord who healed Naaman. To accept payment from Naaman would have meant that Elisha had healed him through medication. He would have robbed God of His honor and deprived Naaman of the joy of honoring God. When Gehazi took the gift, he dishonored God. That was the root of the problem; he did not care about the honor of God, and therefore he had no respect for Naaman, for the prophet, and for himself. All was not well with him.

CONCLUSION

Is all well with you? The question addresses our inner condition, our wholeness or lack of it. Sin by nature fractures us, fragments us. We become like particles moving in different directions, propelled by our inner selfish concerns. Gehazi was concerned about the future and tried to take it into his own hands. Consequently, his peace was gone. Not everything was well with him. It is only when we understand that no matter what we may be going through now or what we may anticipate about the future, our future is in God's hands. We can only learn to live at peace with others and with ourselves by receiving wholeness from God. In this story Gehazi stands for those who deny their lack of wellness, while Naaman represents those who have found shalom in the healing power of God and joy in disinterested service to others and to God, who cares for others. Such lives are characterized by humility and love. They walk or travel on the way of the Lord. You have experienced healing; all should be well with you. But if by any chance you feel that not everything is well, would you like for us to pray for you this morning that you will experience the wellness that only Christ can give us and that comes to us through the gift of divine forgiveness?

Man, created for fellowship with God, can only in such fellowship find his real life and development. Created to find in God his highest joy, he can find in nothing else that which can quiet the cravings of the heart, can satisfy the hunger and thirst of the soul. He who with sincere and teachable spirit studies God's word, seeking to comprehend its truths, will be brought in touch with its Author; and, except by his own choice, there is no limit to the possibilities of his development.[2]

---

[2] Ellen G. White, *Education* (Pacific Press, 1903), 124-125.

CHAPTER 10

IN BEHOLDING HIM, I AM CHANGED!

Artur A. Stele

Psalm 43 is very closely connected thematically, structurally, and linguistically to Psalm 42. In fact, both Psalms have identical refrains. Psalm 42 has two stanzas, and each one has a refrain. However, Psalm 43 has only one stanza and one refrain. The refrains of these two Psalms are almost word for word identical. Psalm 43 does not have a separate title, which actually can signal that it is to be considered as a unit together with Psalm 42. It is important to note the close relationship of these two Psalms right from the beginning, because it will reveal some richness in the meaning, as we will see along the way.

These two Psalms deal with a condition in which human beings find themselves quite often, especially when things go differently than hoped or planned, when we find ourselves in an environment that is not friendly toward us and are in a state of depression, a spiritual depression. The very fact that one of the most often repeated words is the question "Why?" speaks for itself. In fact, in our Bible passage this question "why" occurs no less than 10 times: six times in Psalm 42, and four times in Psalm 43. In addition, Psalm 42 poses three other questions: twice it asks the question "where?" and once the question "when?" In fact, the Psalmist states in 42:3: "They say to me all day long, 'Where is your God?'"[1] If you trusted God, why have these things happened to you? Where is your God? Although the Psalmist uses this question "where" only two times, he states explicitly that he hears this question all day long, continuously: Where? Why? When?

---

[1] Unless otherwise indicated, Scripture quotations are from the New American Standard Bible, 1995 edition.

Don't we also hear or actually ask ourselves very often the same questions: Where was God when bad things happened to me? Why? Why me? Or in a different circumstance we cry out to the Lord: "Why not me, O Lord?" The more we ask these questions—the more we concentrate on the problems and challenges—the more likely it is that we will experience depression.

The longer we are occupied with the problem, the lonelier we become. The longer we concentrate our attention on the problems, the more our pain progresses, becoming worse and worse. The challenges we see appear more forceful with every new glance at them. This we can see very clearly while comparing Psalm 42:9 with Psalm 43:2.

Psalm 42:9 says, "'Why have You forgotten me?'" But little later, in Psalm 43:2, we hear the same question but describing the situation even more strongly. It asks, "'Why have You rejected me?'" Here we clearly see a progression. As the Psalmist contemplated his problems more and more, he moved from the feeling of being forgotten to the feeling of being totally rejected! The silence of God, His apparent absence, makes the situation intolerable.

In fact, there seems to be some irony in the fact that in 42:6, in speaking to God, the Psalmist makes it clear: "I remember You," but in verse 9 he continues addressing God with the plaintive question, "'Why have You forgotten me?'" Later, in 43:2, he seems to be saying, "You have not only forgotten but actually rejected me, but I remember You!" We can almost hear him say, "Lord, is it fair?"

Psalm 42:9 continues: "'Why do I go mourning because of the oppression of the enemy?'"

Then when we come to Psalm 43:2, the same question is raised before God again: "Why do I go mourning because of the oppression of the enemy?" Although the same words are used in both Psalms, the verb for "mourning" in Hebrew has a different grammatical form in Psalm 43, changing the meaning to: "Why do I go **continually** mourning because of the oppression of the enemy?" We see clearly here a progression from bad to worse. As long as God remains silent, the anguish becomes unbearable!

Psalm 43 starts with a cry in a courtroom. It actually presents a courtroom scene. The Psalmist starts the Psalm with a cry that translates literally, "Judge me, O God!" One would expect a cry that would go somewhat along the lines of "Please, help me, Lord!" But instead, we hear, "Judge me, God!"

1. Vindicate me, O God, and plead my case against an ungodly nation; O deliver me from the deceitful and unjust man!

2. For You are the God of my strength; why have You rejected me?

Why do I go **continually** mourning because of the oppression of the enemy?

This is only possible because the Psalmist had a correct picture of God. He understood very clearly that his God is not only the supreme judge but also the One who alone can defend and vindicate. However, all this knowledge has not yet changed the mood of the Psalmist.

It is of great significance to note that the Psalm ends before the refrain with a totally different scene. It is actually a very joyful scene. One can almost call it a feast, a celebration scene. Verse 4:

"Then I will go to the altar of God,

To God my exceeding joy;

And upon the lyre I shall praise You, O God, my God."

There is no sign of depression, no sign of discouragement or hopelessness anymore, but rather a very jubilant atmosphere. Here the Psalmist speaks about an exceeding joy. He shouts in exultation and finds himself in a state of jubilation and rejoicing. And yet words are not enough to express his joy, so he takes a musical instrument, a lyre, and he joyfully praises his God, calling Him "*my* God"!

What made the difference?

Essentially it is verse 3 that made all the difference: "O send out Your light and Your truth, let them lead me; Let them bring me to Your holy hill and to your dwelling places." Let them bring me closer to my God!

He started in a depressed and mourning mood, still feeling rejected, and yet he finished on an exceedingly joyful chord. What made the difference? What was the cure?

One writer stated it well:

The most miserable Christians are those who know Christ (and I may add, even have the right theology) but are not living in Him (with Him). *They have the worst of both worlds.* They can no longer be satisfied in their old life, yet neither are they satisfied in the Lord.[2]

They are miserable themselves and also make all those who surround them miserable. Even in their orthodoxy they misrepresent the One with whom they really are not acquainted.

It is very unfortunate that a significant number if not the majority of Christians live in this condition—so to speak, *in between.* And as a result, they have the worst of both worlds. They have not tasted the true joy of being a child of God! The tragedy of the situation is, if you have not tasted fellowship with God, a close friendship with Him, you can be a very knowledgeable person, even a pastor or theologian, and yet reject Christ Himself. Just remember the first coming of Christ. Who rejected Him? Very religious people, even the spiritual leaders. Why? Because they lacked that genuine relationship with God.

The Psalmist discovered the cure. This why he is crying out, "O send out Your light and Your Truth, let them lead me; Let them bring me to Your holy hill and to your dwelling places." Let them bring me closer to my God!

Possibly the psalmist reflects here on the wilderness experience, reminding himself of the pillar of fire keeping Israel through the desolate and harsh environment during the night and the pillar of cloud guiding, protecting, and providing comfort during the day when the sun was scorching everything that had life in the wilderness.

---

[2] Donald M. Williams, *The Communicator's Commentary. Psalms 1-72* (Waco, Texas: Word Books Publisher, 1986), 317.

The Psalmist is pleading for God's light and His truth. He understands them as the necessary companions on the way home to the dwelling places of God Himself—to the places he longs for like the deer longs for flowing streams: "As a deer pants for the water brooks, so my soul pants for You, O God. My soul thirsts for God, for the living God; When shall I come and appear before God?" (Ps 42:1-2).

"O send out thy light and thy truth: let them lead me; let them bring me unto thy holy hill, and to thy tabernacles" (Ps 43:3, KJV).

God Himself is the goal of the journey. The holy hill, God's dwellings, the sanctuary and the altar are but the means of approaching Him and enjoying His presence.

God's light and His truth! These are the elements that make all the difference. These are the vehicles that can bring us to the place we long for.

So, what is God's truth?

In John 17:17, Jesus prays for us: "'Sanctify them in the truth; Your word is truth.'" The word!

It is interesting to note, however, that the Psalmist is asking not only for the Word but also for the Light.

He knows too well that we can be lost in interpreting the Word. So he is asking for Light also.

> In these days of peril we should be exceedingly careful not to reject the rays of light which Heaven in mercy sends us, for it is by these that we are to discern the devices of the enemy. We need light from Heaven every hour, that we may distinguish between the sacred and the common, the eternal and the temporal. If left to ourselves, we shall blunder at every step.[3]

Psalm 36:9 states: "In Your light we see light." We cannot even see light if God does not send His light. It is only in His light that we are able to see light! Without His light we might be

---

[3] Ellen G. White, *My Life Today* (Washington, DC: Review and Herald, 1952), 321.

very sure in our way of interpreting scriptures, but our own light is nothing more than darkness when compared to His true light.

No common light can show us the way.

No common light can break the darkness.

No common light can lead us out of our own dead-end hermeneutics.

It is of great importance not to forget that the New Testament **clearly underlines the personification of both the Truth and the Light.**

Jesus is presented in the Gospel of John as the Truth! "I am the Truth," states Jesus (see John 14:6).

"I am the Light of the world" (John 8:12).

There is no truth without Jesus, and there is no Jesus without the Truth.

The cry, "O send out Your light and Your truth," is actually the call, "O, give me Jesus!"

If we don't have Jesus, if we are not in Him, then we have not experienced the joy of being His children.

Then we have the worst of both worlds. We "are neither cold nor hot."

And what about Jesus? He says: "Behold, I stand at the door and knock."

If we open the door, everything changes:

Darkness and gloom cannot stand Jesus! Error and fault cannot stand Him!

If you have Jesus, everything changes:
The night turns into day.
The darkness turns into light.
The Judge into a Defender.
A judgment hall into a sanctuary.
Enemies into instruments of our growth.
Crying and weeping into a song.

Sadness into joy.
Mourning into praise.
A downcast soul into a joyful person.

When Jesus comes in, everything changes! Not only our understanding! Not only our feelings and mood!

Not only how we relate to others, not only how we speak to and value those who think differently than we do, but also our appearance—even our face changes!

Let's look at the refrain in Psalms 42 and 43:

42:5
Why are you in despair, O my soul?
And why have you become disturbed within me?
Hope in God, for I shall again praise Him
For the help of His presence. [Here it literally says,
The salvation of His face.]

You are concerned, asking, "What will people think about my God, about why He is allowing this and that happen to me? They are asking, 'Where is your God?'"

Do not worry. He says, "I will take care of it. I will vindicate myself."

Psalms 42:11, 43:5:
Why are you in despair, O my soul?
And why are you disturbed within me?
Hope in God, for I shall again praise Him,
The help of my countenance and my God." Here it
literally says: The salvation of my face.
He will save my face. But there is another nuance as well:

In beholding Him, my face changes.

While we dwell in His Word, remaining in His Light, we are becoming transformed in such a way that Jesus says: Now "you are the light of the world" (John 5:14). Your life, your actions, your words, yes, even your face will witness, will show, will demonstrate who your father is!

I will never forget my time of serving a little over two years in the Soviet military. The strategy of the Soviet brainwashing machine was such that Christian young boys were taken from their homes and sent several thousand kilometers away, so that nobody could visit them. Then, in that faraway place, they would make sure that no two believers were in the same unit. In the beginning, daily and sometimes twice a day, they were checking our pockets, our mail, and our belongings to make sure that no Bibles or any religious materials would be with us, and they would brainwash us hour after hour, telling us that "you are the only believer in the world, besides your family and several grandmothers that never had a decent education. Normal modern people do not believe in God, because He does not exist." The interrogation went on for hours each day.

One day a new military unit visited our unit for several hours, only to have lunch. We were standing in a big hall in the cafeteria as the new unit marched in. As they walked in, in this large crowd of solders I suddenly noticed a face—a face that I had never seen before. He was a total stranger to me, but yet his face was different. I started silently walking toward him, and he also started to move toward me. As I came close enough to him, I asked him a question: "Are you a believer?" At the same time, he was asking me the same question: "Are you are a Christian?" We found a quiet place, we prayed together, and we strengthened each other with some Bible texts that we had memorized. Our faces had become a sermon.

"O send out Your light and Your truth, let them lead me."

CHAPTER 11

DIVINE COMPASSION

Ángel Manuel Rodríguez

There is an element of mystery in the story we read, yet it is indeed a very simple story. It addresses the issue of death, but its central theme is life. We find in it sadness and suffering, but its main interest is joy and gladness. This is a story of love. It is not the story of a mother, her child, and the Lord. It is somehow the story of the human race. This is our story. I am in it; you are also in it. Please allow me to tell you this wonderful story of love, sacrifice, and triumph.

We do not know how it happened, but all we know is that this woman's son, her only son, died. Not long before, her husband had died. Since then, she saw in her son her only treasure, her hope for the future. She cared for him; she provided for him; she loved him. She dreamed about the time when her son would become a great man in Israel. She felt secure, knowing that in the future her son would take care of her, providing for her needs.

But the young man died. His eyes were closed; his body was washed with aromatics and scents, wrapped in a shroud, his face veiled with a sudarium, and his hands and feet tied with linen strips. The young man was taken to the upper room of the house, where relatives and friends were to come to express their sympathy to the widow. He had to be buried within eight hours.

A few hours later the coffin was brought into the house. It was not actually a coffin; rather, it was an open bier, a litter. Those passing by could see the body of the young boy. The time to take the widow's son to the burial place had come, and the mother could not control herself any longer. When she saw her only son being carried out from her house to the narrow streets of Nain, a loud cry of pain and desperation came out of her heart.

THE MYSTERY OF REDEMPTION

DISHARMONY: TWO CROWDS

The streets were filled with noise, the noise of death. The funeral procession was quickly organized. Heading the procession was the widow, dressed in sackcloth, indicating that she was a widow. She was crying very loudly; she was grief-stricken. Behind her one could see the professional mourners, ladies paid to show grief. They were uttering piercing cries throughout the whole length of the journey. Most probably this time they were not crying simply because they were being paid; they cried because they could fully identify with the widow.

Usually a group of musicians formed part of the funeral procession. They played laments; the sound of sadness came out of their instruments. Farther behind, one could see a group of men carrying the open bier. On it was placed the corpse of the only son of the widow. This crowd was heading to the gate of the village of Nain.

But there was something the widow did not know; a few hours before she began her funeral procession, another crowd had left from the city of Capernaum, and it was heading toward the village of Nain. This crowd was completely different from the previous one. They were walking together, talking and praising the Lord. At the front of this crowd, and determining its direction, was Jesus. He walked with authority, His head high, and His steps firm. He was not followed by a coffin but by His disciples and a large number of people who had been healed by Him. Some of them had been liberated from the power of demons. They followed Jesus out of gratitude and love.

Luke is describing for us two different crowds. One is characterized by sadness and pain, the other by joy and happiness. The ugliness of death and the absence of power are located at the very center of one of them; the other has in its center the beauty of life and the presence of power. In one of them the action was determined by what had happened to the only son, the *monogenés*, of the widow; in the other crowd the action was determined by what the only son of God, the *monogenés*, had done on behalf of others. In the first crowd the son was a passive recipient; in the second the Son was a dynamic agent. The two crowds were to meet each other. They both were heading to the gate of the city.

The reference to "the gate of the city" (Luke 7:12, NKJV) suggests that Nain was a walled city, probably protected by strong fortresses, which was strange for a small village. In the ancient world, the purpose of the wall and the gate was to protect the citizens. In case of a military attack they could find security and protection inside the city. Thus were their lives to be preserved. Every night the gates were closed. The people went to sleep feeling secure.

Yet, for the widow of Nain neither the walls nor the fortresses nor the gate provided peace, tranquility, or security. Death passed through the walls, the fortresses, and the gate; it ran through the streets of the village and for a second time had gone into her house. There was one more victim, her only son.

Human life cannot be preserved through human inventions. Our most powerful efforts cannot give us abundant life. This story is precisely about our greatest need, about our lack of power, which frustrates our deepest wishes and most glorious dreams.

ENCOUNTER: THE CROWDS MEET

Jesus was close enough to see the gate of the city. As He came closer, His ear, sensitive to the human cry for help, captured the noise of the other crowd. He realized that this was a crowd characterized by misery and pain. He stopped, and those following him kept quiet. They could all hear the cries of suffering and death.

Their eyes were fixed on the gate of the city. The first person to appear was the widow. Her hair was disarranged, she cast herself down to the ground, gathered dust and threw it up in the air; she stood up, hit her chest and loudly shouted. She was desperate, hopeless.

The story says, "When the Lord saw her, . . . " (Luke 7:13).[1] It does not say "Jesus saw her," "Christ saw her," "the Savior saw her." The one who saw her was the *kurios*, the Lord, the one whose Lordship is eternal. In Him there is not a fragment of impotence. Notice that power and security are not located inside the city. The

---

[1] Scripture quotations not otherwise designated are from the New International Version.

fortified city is a symbol of human achievements and inventions. Power was located outside of it. It is there where our power is located.

The Lord saw this woman as no other could see her. She was destined to extinction, to forgetfulness, to misery. Her memory was going to be erased from the face of the earth. She did not have a husband who could provide a future for her; and now the only possibility of a meaningful future, her son, was gone. The death of her son was indeed her own death, and she demonstrated it through her mourning ritual. The Lord saw her just as she was: poor and needy. She could only share with Him her misery.

When He saw her, "his heart went out to her." Jesus' being was shaken at its very center. Love wanted to express itself. This love was not created by the woman's need. This love is the controlling power of God's actions and is born in the mystery of God's being. Our redemption is a mystery because it was born in the inscrutable depth of God's love.

Life and death are going to confront each other face to face. A new chapter in the cosmic conflict is about to be written. Will God's love be powerful enough to save us, to deliver us from the power of death? God's love is active. Jesus walked toward the woman. She probably saw Him, but that did not stop her crying. Jesus took a closer look at the woman: suffering and pain had incarnated themselves in her.

HARMONY THROUGH THE SON: ONE CROWD
Then from the lips of the Lord came some brief words: "Do not cry." She was being comforted by the Savior! I have thought about this many times. I have also cried, many times and in different places, and it would have been wonderful in those occasions to feel the touch of the Lord on my shoulder and to hear Him saying to me, "Ángel, do not cry." But, reading this story I realized that what He said to the widow He was also saying to me.

The words of Jesus were not just a request; they were a promise. To ask someone who is crying to stop crying is meaningless unless we have the power to remove the cause for the crying. Jesus was promising her that He was going to remove the cause of her tears. Jesus' request to the widow is a promise to the human race.

There is a constant cry going up from this planet to heaven. There are people crying for help right now while someone attempts to kill or rape or rob them. No one who comes to this planet leaves it without dropping a tear. In fact, one of the common characteristics of human beings is that we all cry. Jesus is telling us that the time is coming when human pain and suffering will end. He is going to remove from our planet the source of death and suffering.

How could that happen? It happens through the power of His sacrifice. Jesus was about to do something amazing, even disconcerting, baffling. What He was going to do was to be done on behalf of that widow, who had no future and who had also realized that there was no security at all in human accomplishments and achievements. She had discovered the futility of human effort. From this powerless person who had nothing to offer, nothing was asked. Instead the Lord offered her comfort, even a promise: "Do not cry, I am going to remove the cause of your misery."

Those carrying the open bier were coming. Jesus left the woman and walked toward them. They were carrying the symbol of impurity *par excellence,* of absolute and complete separation from God: death. Jesus was not afraid of it, for as the Lord, He had power over it. He stretched out His arm and touched the bier, the unclean. The men carrying it stopped. The Lord who was purity and holiness in human form, God incarnate, came into direct contact with death. This was the touch of interchange and substitution.

2 Cor 5:21 "God made him who had no sin to be sin for us, so that in him we might become the righteousness of God."

If the widow is to stop crying, it must be because someone else will cry in her place. This is an illustration, a parable, of the mystery of redemption. Holiness and impurity confronted each other, and in an unfathomable way they touched each other. It was at the cost of that confrontation that we were redeemed.

"Young man, I say to you, get up!" The Lord was talking to a corpse! I have seen people talking to a dead person: a wife asking her dead husband why he left her; a mother telling her dead child how much she loved him. But the dead could not hear them. Yet, Christ's voice was powerful to penetrate the darkness of death, shaking up the dead body. The vital power of God raised him up.

He was alive! Yes, the only son of the widow was alive, only because the Only Son of God is going to die in his place.

The young man sat on the bier, probably asking himself what was going on. He began to talk; we do not know what he said, but I can imagine that after seeing his mother he simply shouted, "Mother!" Perhaps she heard his voice and possibly said to herself, "Oh Lord, I am hearing the voice of my son. I must be hallucinating. We both know that he is dead." While she was wondering about the voice she was hearing, Jesus took the young man by the hand and brought him to the woman. He gave back to this woman life, joy, and a glorious future.

Death was defeated, and suffering and pain were extinguished. The crowd from the village was transformed and possessed by the joy that characterized the crowd from Capernaum. A glorious miracle had taken place: the two crowds merged into one! The encounter resulted in harmony, because death was overcome by the only Son of God.

CONCLUSION

We were made by God to live eternally. We lost that possibility, but God gave us life again through Christ. Life is not the result of human achievements. It is found in the rejection of those efforts and in the acceptance of what God has done for us in Jesus. The experience of the widow and her son is our experience, and her suffering and misery are also ours.

Jesus continues to be the powerful Lord who is also our Savior by taking our place. Soon the last aspect of the plan of redemption, its consummation, will become a reality. We will hear again the voice of our Lord calling His servants back to life. Friends and relatives will be united once more in indissoluble bonds of love.

There is going to be, instead of two crowds, only one crowd. We will all be praising the Lord, and there will be perfect harmony throughout the universe. We must start praising Him now for what He has done. We may not be able to penetrate the mystery of redemption, but we can start enjoying it now and today. Above all, we should proclaim from the depths of our hearts that soon and very soon Jesus, at His Second Coming, will eliminate from the universe suffering and death.

CHAPTER 12

THE TOUCH OF HOPE

Elias Brasil de Souza

"Every miracle in the Bible first started as a problem!"[1] The truth of this aphorism suitably applies to the miracle that Jesus performed for a woman who touched the hem of His garment. This miracle certainly made a profound impression on the Gospel writers since it appears in Matthew (9:20-22), Mark (5:25-34), and Luke (8:43-48). This is how Mark recounts the story:

> Now a certain woman had a flow of blood for twelve years, and had suffered many things from many physicians. She had spent all that she had and was no better, but rather grew worse. When she heard about Jesus, she came behind Him in the crowd and touched His garment. For she said, "If only I may touch His clothes, I shall be made well." Immediately the fountain of her blood was dried up, and she felt in her body that she was healed of the affliction. And Jesus, immediately knowing in Himself that power had gone out of Him, turned around in the crowd and said, "Who touched My clothes?" But His disciples said to Him, "You see the multitude thronging You, and You say, 'Who touched Me?'" And He looked around to see her who had done this thing. But the woman, fearing and trembling, knowing what had happened to her, came and fell down before Him and

---

[1] This aphorism appears in many places on the Internet with no ascriptions. It appears, e.g., in https://flowersontherubbishheap.wordpress.com/2016/05/01/every-miracle-started-with-a-problem/ (accessed October 11, 2021). and in other places on the Internet, but with no ascription.

told Him the whole truth. And He said to her, "Daughter, your faith has made you well. Go in peace, and be healed of your affliction" (Mark 5:25-34).[2]

THE CONTEXT

Our story lies inside the story of the resurrection of Jairus's daughter. In the previous verses, the text reports the request of Jairus, head of Capernaum synagogue. Jairus came to Jesus with a desperate request for Jesus to heal his 12-year-old daughter (Mark 5:42). But on His journey to Jairus's home, Jesus stops to attend to the woman with the flow of blood. After healing the woman, Jesus resumes going to Jairus's house, where He performs another miracle by bringing Jairus's daughter back to life. So, the story of the woman with the flow of blood is placed inside the story related to Jairus. This is a common literary device used in the Gospel of Mark, called "sandwich stories."[3] Mark begins to tell a story, then tells another story, and finally resumes the first story and concludes it. Close attention to this context provides interesting insights into our story.

THE PROBLEM

The story begins with Jairus's desperate plea to Jesus: "'My little daughter lies at the point of death. Come and lay Your hands on her, that she may be healed, and she will live'" (Mark 5:23). Immediately, Jesus began to walk toward Jairus's home, accompanied by a large crowd. However, amid the crowd that followed the Master, there was a woman just as desperate as Jairus. She had been suffering from a flow of blood for 12 years (Matt 9:20; Luke 8:43). That is, during the entire time in which

---

[2] Unless otherwise indicated, Scripture quotations are from the New King James Version.

[3] As Gregory K. Hollifield, "Pericope-By-Pericope: Transforming Disciples Into Christ's Likeness Through the Theological Interpretation of Scripture," *Journal for Baptist Theology and Ministry* 15/1 (2018): 59, explains: "Biblical authors in both testaments often 'sandwich' stories within stories to make more than one point at a time. Naaman's healing and generosity, in contrast to Gehazi's greed and subsequent leprosy (2 Kings 5), are sandwiched within the larger Elisha narrative (2 Kings 2-8). Mark's Gospel contains six sandwich stories, most notably the story about Jesus's healing of the woman with the bloody issue sandwiched within the account of His raising Jairus's daughter." See also, Tom Shepherd, *Markan Sandwich Stories: Narration, Definition, and Function* (Berrien Springs, MI: Andrews University Press, 1993).

Jairus's daughter had been living, this woman had been suffering. Our text says that she "had suffered many things from many physicians. She had spent all that she had and was no better, but rather grew worse" (Mark 5:26). It is interesting to note that Luke—perhaps because he was a physician!—does not mention the word "physicians," but limits himself to saying that she "could not be healed by any" (Luke 8:43).

Indeed, some streams of rabbinic tradition expressed many reservations about physicians. As the Talmud says: "R[abbi] Judah says in his name, 'Most ass drivers are evil, most camel drivers are decent, most sailors are saintly, *the best among physicians is going to Gehenna*, and the best of butchers is a partner of Amalek.'"[4] Of course, we should bear in mind that ancient physicians did not practice science-based medicine. As one author put it, "The story of early medicine is one of magic and sorcery, religion and prayers, shamans and surgeons, ingenuity and experimentation."[5]

Curiously, the Talmud itself lists no fewer than eleven cures for such a trouble, which gives us an idea of what kinds of "medical" treatments that woman may have tried:

> Bring the weight of a zuz[6] of Alexandrian gum, a zuz weight of liquid alum, and a zuz weight of garden crocus; powder them together. For a woman affected with flux uncleanness, a mixture of a third of that with wine helps for her not to become barren. . . .

> For a woman affected with flux uncleanness, a mixture of a third of that with wine helps for her not to become barren: but if not, then bring three [110B] qapiza[7] measures of Persian onions and boil them in wine and give the mixture to her to drink, saying, "Stop your flux."

[4] Jacob Neusner, *The Babylonian Talmud: A Translation and Commentary* (Peabody, MA: Hendrickson, 2011), 12:403, emphasis added.

[5] Kate Kelly, *The History of Medicine: Early Civilizations: Prehistoric Times to 500 C.E.* (New York: Facts On File, 2009), xiv.

[6] Zuz is "a silver coin equivalent to a silver dinar," as noted by David Instone-Brewer, *Traditions of the Rabbis from the Era of the New Testament, Volume 1, Prayer and Agriculture* (Grand Rapids, MI: Eerdmans, 2004), 430.

[7] Kapiza equals a tenth of an ephah (2.18 liters) according to Angelo Segrè, "Babylonian, Assyrian and Persian Measures," *Journal of the American Oriental Society* 64/2 (1944): 76.

But if not, sit her at a crossroads, put a cup of wine in her hand, and someone comes up from behind and frightens her and exclaims, "Stop your flux."

But if not, bring a handful of cumin, a handful of saffron, and a handful of fenugreek and boil them in wine. Let her drink it; and they say to her, "Stop your flux."

But if not, bring sixty pieces of sealing clay of a wine vessel and let them smear her with it and say to her, "Stop your flux."

But if not, bring a thistle growing among Roman thorns, burn it, collect linen rags in summer or cotton rags in winter.

But if not, bring a fern, boil it in wine, smear her with it, and say to her, "Stop your flux."

But if not, dig seven holes and burn in them a young shoot of produce of a fruit tree in the first three years after its planting, put a cup of wine in her hand, make her rise from one hole and seat her on the next, and do the same for the rest, and at each point say to her, "Stop your flux."

But if not, bring fine flour, rub her from the lower half downwards, and say to her, "Stop your flux."

But if not, bring an ostrich egg, burn it and wrap it in linen rags in summer or cotton rags in winter.

But if not, break open a barrel of wine especially for her.

But if not, bring barley grain found in the dung of a white mule; if she holds it for one day, her discharge will cease for two days, if she holds it for two, it will cease for three, if she holds it for three days, it will cease forever.[8]

That woman was not only carrying the pain of the physical suffering; she also suffered the emotional torment of discrimination and segregation. Anything or anyone she touched would have been considered unclean. So, she could not mix with people

---

[8] Neusner, *Babylonian Talmud*, 2:499–500.

in public lest she contaminate them. She could not go to the synagogue or the courtyard of the women in the temple because she was impure; nor could she marry, since she would contaminate her husband. If by chance she did get married, the man would possibly be forced to divorce her. She could not work around other people because of the danger of contamination. This may have reduced her to a life of begging at the margins of society.

Within the framework of the ceremonial law, her situation was clear:

> If a woman has a discharge of blood for many days, other than at the time of her customary impurity, or if it runs beyond her usual time of impurity, all the days of her unclean discharge shall be as the days of her customary impurity. She shall be unclean. Every bed on which she lies all the days of her discharge shall be to her as the bed of her impurity; and whatever she sits on shall be unclean, as the uncleanness of her impurity (Lev 15:25-26).

That woman stands as an apt representative of humanity groaning under the weight of sin and suffering. As we look around the world today, we see pain, despair, violence, and sin. But as we follow the story, we note that there is still hope in a hopeless world.

THE HEALING

This woman had heard of Jesus. We do not know who told her. Maybe it was someone who had been healed by touching Jesus' clothes. We learn from the Gospel of Luke that many people received healing by touching Jesus: "And the whole multitude sought to touch Him, because power went out from Him and healed them all" (Luke 6:19). As she heard about these stories, the conviction grew within her that if she only could touch the garment of the Master, she could achieve in an instant what those 12 long years of humiliation, suffering, and expensive treatments at the hands of many doctors had been unable to provide.

What a contrast between the faith of the woman and the faith of Jairus! Whereas the head of the synagogue wanted Jesus to come to his house and heal his daughter, the woman, considering herself unworthy of the attention of Jesus, believed that if she could only touch His garment, she would be healed. In fact, both have shown great faith, but the faith of the woman seems to have run deeper. It may have been superstitious, but whatever difficulties she had in understanding such matters, the fact of the matter is, she placed her faith in the right Person. One commentator noted:

> The woman's faith was at its core an ignorant faith. She sought a cure that was essentially magic-secured (touching the edge of his robe). She had no idea that Jesus would know anything about what she did. Her faith was uninformed, presumptuous, and superstitious, but it was *real*, and Christ honored her imperfect faith.
>
> God still does the same thing today. Beginning faith is often uninformed and mixed with many errors about, for example, Christ's person, the Incarnation, the Trinity, the Atonement, grace/works, the Scriptures, etc. However, such foggy understandings are often the beginning of a deep, informed trust in God. We can take courage in this. One does not need to have it all figured out to possess a faith which pleases God. This is why a child can come to Christ. This is why God often saves those who know virtually no theology. This does not minimize deep understanding, which is meant to foster a profound faith. The point is, a faith that pleases God does not belong only to the informed elite.[9]

It bears noting that the woman showed courage to approach Jesus because as she made her way through the crowd to reach Jesus, she was technically contaminating everyone. She risked being recognized; if so, she would have been exposed to public humiliation and ridicule with possible punishment. However, the risk was worth taking because she believed that Jesus could restore her, if she could only touch His garments.

---

[9] R. Kent Hughes, *Mark: Jesus, Servant and Savior* (Westchester, IL: Crossway, 1989), 128.

And getting close enough to Jesus, or as the parallel text of Matthew says, coming "from behind," she "touched the hem of His garment" (Matt 9:20). The hem of Jesus' garment most likely was the four blue tassels worn on the mantle by devout Jews in accordance with the law of Moses. As one commentator explained:

> Every devout Jew wore an outer robe with four tassels on it, one at each corner. These tassels were worn in obedience to the command in Numbers 15:38-40, and they were to signify to others, and to remind the man himself, that the wearer was a member of the chosen people of God. They were the badge of a devout Jew.[10]

By touching the hem of Jesus' garment, the woman received in an instant what all the physicians' therapies had failed to provide during her 12 years of suffering. She touched Jesus' garment; Jesus touched her life.

It does not matter how long you have been struggling with some addiction, troubling relationships, family issues, health issues, or sin. Come to Jesus. In Him there is healing, power, and forgiveness.

Upon touching the Master's garment, she immediately felt a transformation in her body and realized that everything would be different from that moment on. As our passage says, "the woman, fearing and trembling, knowing what had happened to her, came and fell down before Him and told Him the whole truth" (Mark 5:33). We do not know exactly what that "truth" was. It may be that she told Jesus about her suffering and hope of finding healing. Or probably she simply "confesses her daring act."[11] But whatever she may have told Jesus, it important to note that she told the "whole truth." She did not hide anything from Jesus. Her commitment was complete.[12] As we go to Jesus, let us not forget to tell Him the "whole truth" about our challenges, needs, sufferings, and sins. In Jesus we find power, healing, and forgiveness.

---

[10] William Barclay, *The New Daily Study Bible: The Gospel of Mark* (Edinburgh: Saint Andrew Press, 2001), 150.

[11] Mary Healy, *The Gospel of Mark: Catholic Commentary on Sacred Scripture* (Grand Rapids, MI: Baker, 2008), 106.

[12] Donald English, *The Message of Mark: The Mystery of Faith* (Downers Grove, IL: InterVarsity Press, 1992), 115.

Coming back to the story, let us see how Ellen White beautifully notes Jesus' compassionate response to that suffering woman:

> Christ knew every thought of her mind, and He was making His way to where she stood. He realized her great need, and He was helping her to exercise faith.
>
> As He was passing, she reached forward and succeeded in barely touching the border of His garment. That moment she knew that she was healed. *In that one touch was concentrated the faith of her life, and instantly her pain and feebleness disappeared.* Instantly she felt the thrill as of an electric current passing through every fiber of her being. There came over her a sensation of perfect health.[13]

Jesus was not afraid of defilement. According to the ceremonial law, uncleanness usually predominates over purity (Hag 2:12-13). That is, when the unclean touches a clean object or person, the clean becomes unclean, so that when purity confronts impurity, impurity prevails. But there is one exception: when an unclean object came into contact with a source of water, a source of living water cannot be contaminated; it was immune to impurity (Lev 11:36). So Jesus, as a source of living water (John 7:37-39) springing purity, love, and forgiveness, could not be made unclean by the touch of an impure woman. Nothing could defile Him; rather, when the woman's impurity came in contact with the holiness of Jesus, the Master released a power that healed, cleansed, and restored that woman (Mark 5:30).

THE FAITH

She got more than physical healing that day: she got spiritual healing—she received salvation. The saving intervention and love of Jesus in the life of the woman is accompanied by a sweet declaration of divine love, unparalleled in other reports of healings and miracles of Jesus: "'Daughter, your faith has made you well. Go in peace, and be healed of your affliction'" (Mark 5:34).

---

[13] Ellen G. White, *The Ministry of Healing* (Mountain View, CA: Pacific Press, 1905), 60, emphasis added.

Two points deserve reflection. First, Jesus called her "daughter." Strikingly, this "is the only time Jesus addresses someone as 'daughter.'"[14] Why so? Maybe Jesus calls her daughter to justify the delay in attending to Jairus's request. As the woman came and touched the garment of Jesus, she caused a momentary interruption in Jesus' journey to the house of Jairus, where a dying girl was waiting for the healing intervention of the Great Physician. We can imagine that, perhaps for a few moments, the father, stricken by the fear of losing his daughter, may have felt irritated with that situation that prevented Jesus from keeping on going to his house. So, in calling that woman "daughter," Jesus seems to suggest that while the daughter of Jairus needed urgent help, this other "daughter" also needed help. Perhaps the message for Jairus was something like this: "Jairus, you have a 12-year-old daughter who needs help, but before helping your daughter, I need to help this woman, who is My daughter, and who has been suffering for 12 years."

Second, Jesus highlights the faith of this woman: "Your faith has saved you." Among the crowd, there were many people who thronged around Jesus and pressed Him. Thus, when Jesus felt the touch of the woman on His garment and asked who had touched Him, the disciples reacted with astonishment—the question seemed silly. After all, walking among a crowd, what sense would there be in Jesus' question, "Who touched me?" (Mark 5:30). In fact, many people surrounded Jesus and touched him, but it was the touch of curiosity. Many people were there just out of curiosity; their journey with Jesus would end at Jairus's house. They would bear witness of Jesus' life-giving power in raising Jairus's daughter, but with their curiosity satisfied, they would return to business as usual.

But Jesus asked who touched Him, because He felt that someone had touched Him, not only with the body or hands, but with the heart. In this woman's touch the Master felt the despair of a human being who came to Him as her last and only hope of restoration, healing, and forgiveness. It was the touch of faith and surrender. And the woman received what she had craved during

---

[14] R. T. France, *Luke*, ed. Mark L. Strauss and John H. Walton, Teach the Text Commentary Series (Grand Rapids, MI: Baker, 2013), 154.

those 12 years of pain and suffering. She received physical restoration: the flow of blood, which had drained her physical strength and even her life itself, now ceased. She was no longer a rejected, abandoned, neglected woman, discriminated against by everyone. She had become a daughter of Jesus. She had encountered "the Sun of Righteousness . . . with healing in His wings" (Mal 4:2), and she came out of that encounter transformed.

CONCLUSION

My dear friend, the poor woman of our story

represents humanity—all of us. We are ill. We have spent our resources trying remedies which do not work. Christ comes to us from the Cross. We need to touch him by faith. Do not fear that he will not respond. Do not fear that you are too ignorant. Do not fear that you are too selfish. Fear only one thing—that you will let him pass without reaching out in faith to him.[15]

Jesus alone is able to stop the flow of blood that exhausts the spiritual energies of your life. Only Jesus is able to heal the pain, the grief, or the trauma that has taken such a heavy toll on you. Jesus can forgive that sin that afflicts your conscience and give you the power to live a renewed life. Reach out and touch Jesus. Touch the hem of His garment. Enjoy His comfort, power, peace, strength, and love. Enjoy the hope that only Jesus can provide. Reach out to Jesus, and do not miss the touch of hope in your life!

---

[15] Hughes, *Mark*, 129.

CHAPTER 13

INSIDE THE TOMB OF JESUS

Ángel Manuel Rodríguez

Space is our home. We move from one space to another, but in the final analysis our particular spaces are part of the cosmic space. There are spaces that are very dear to us; we call them places. Perhaps for some of us it is the home where we were born and grew up, or where we met our spouse, or where we studied, or the space that was our first home.

God has also been in different and very strange places. We find Him in the Garden of Eden, on Mount Sinai, in a burning bush, in the temple, in the womb of Mary, and on the cross. Today I invite you to come with me to one of these strange places where God located Himself. It is mentioned in Matthew 27:57-60.

The tomb is probably one of the most important fragments of space in cosmic history. Yes, the cross would be the most important of all of them, but the event of the cross took place on public space. What circumscribed it was cosmic space, making it possible for all to witness the most magnificent display of God's love. The tomb—it was a closed space, a cave, a prison house without an exit. What happened inside it is directly connected to the cross. So, what did happen inside the space we call the tomb of the Son of God? I invite you to come with me and watch. Perhaps, after looking inside this unique space, we will be more grateful to God for making the tomb, at least for a short period of time, His dwelling place. Perhaps we will find there a message of hope and freedom. Come to the tomb of Jesus and see.

INSIDE THE TOMB OF JESUS

OWNER OF THE TOMB

As we enter the tomb, we should probably ask ourselves, Who owns this tomb, this narrow space? We can only answer this question by watching what is taking place inside of it. But the question is a topic of debate outside the tomb. The easiest answer to this most intriguing question would be that it belongs to Joseph of Arimathea; he owns it. But apparently he relinquished his ownership and gave it to the family of Jesus to become a family tomb. Since Joseph is dead, we could assume that the tomb most probably belongs to Mary.

But the Romans would disagree with our assessment of the situation. According to them, the whole land of Israel belongs to them. Therefore, this tomb, they would argue, also belongs to Caesar. In fact, the royal seal had been placed at the very entrance of the tomb, and soldiers had been commanded to guard it in order to make sure that no one would dare to break into a space that was under the control of the Roman authorities. According to them, they own the tomb.

But behind the Roman Empire was an evil spiritual power who was totally convinced that this unique space belongs to him. Satan and a host of his evil angels, demons, surrounded the tomb, claiming that it was theirs. "Hosts of evil angels were gathered about the place. Had it been possible, the prince of darkness with his apostate army would have kept forever sealed the tomb that held the Son of God."[1] After all, did not the realm of death and darkness belong to him?

But there is another person claiming ownership of the tomb. The Father is there while His Son is inside the tomb. Ellen G. White writes, "With majestic and terrible tread, the God of heaven, followed by the angels, walked round the tomb of Christ."[2] God the Father was claiming ownership of the tomb. He walked around it, indicating that this particular space was His. It did not belong to the Roman emperor but to the Emperor of the universe.

---

[1] Ellen G. White, *The Desire of Ages* (Mountain View, CA: Pacific Press, 1898), 779.

[2] *Manuscript Releases*, Vol. 12 (Silver Spring, MD: Ellen G. White Estate, 1990), 421.

The Roman soldiers and Satan and his host could surround the tomb, but far above them the angels of the Lord formed a military cordon to protect the tomb: "A heavenly host surrounded the sepulcher. Angels that excel in strength were guarding the tomb."[3]

Back inside the tomb we see the Son of God, God in human flesh. We could perhaps argue that since He is the dweller in the tomb, He owns it—that He is taking both the tomb and death itself from the hands of the Prince of Darkness and is claiming ownership. But it is difficult to affirm that the Son is the owner, because for now the tomb is His temporal prison house. But things will soon change; they will change on Sunday.

The One inside it was God's Son. On Sunday it would be clear that the tomb was owned by both God and His Son and that it has been under the protection of their angels. Early in the morning, powerful angels pushed aside the powers of darkness and the Roman soldiers and said to the Son of God that it was time for Him to come out. Then the Owner, the Dweller of the house, walked out in all His glory. Christ walked out as the owner. How do we know this? Because, when He left, He took with Him the keys of the house: "I was dead, and behold, I am alive forevermore, and I have the keys of death and of Hades" (Rev 1:18).[4] *It is His empty tomb,* and from now on all tombs belong to Him—including the tomb of your relatives and friends.

PLACE OF LIFE: THE DIVINITY OF JESUS

As we move inside the tomb we see something that should not be there: life. This tomb is a space or place of contrasts. Death brings to an end all activities. It is the ultimate manifestation of de-creation, the dissolution of the order established by God at creation. What was is no longer, and there is only nothingness. The tomb is a place where life is absent. In contrast to that picture, we see inside the tomb Jesus: deity itself, fullness of life. We see there the divinity of the Son of God, the Owner of the tomb. The human and the divine had to remain there for a specific period of time: "He who died for the sins of the world was to remain in the tomb the allotted time. He was in that stony prison house as a

---

[3] White, *The Desire of Ages*, 779.

[4] Unless otherwise indicated, Scripture quotations are from the New American Standard Bible, 1995 edition.

prisoner of divine justice. He was responsible to the Judge of the universe. He was bearing the sins of the world, and His Father only could release Him."[5]

God is by nature dynamic. God, the second person of the Godhead, is alive inside the tomb! And because He is dynamic, He should be doing something. What is He doing there? He is doing what He has always done since creation. Paul, speaking about the work of the pre-incarnated Son of God, states that "He is the image of the invisible God" (Col 1:15). It has been the role of Christ to reveal to all His cosmic intelligent creatures what God is like; He mediated to the cosmos the nature and character of God since the moment of creation. And now from inside the tomb He is telling the cosmos, "Look and see! This is what God is like! God has been willing to descend to the tomb to reveal to all the depths of His sacrificial love toward sinful creatures." A glorious revelation of the love of God was taking place inside the tomb! He did it for us!

While inside the tomb, the Son of God is also performing another aspect of His pre-incarnated work: "He is before all things, and in Him all things hold together" (Col 1:17). He was and continues to be the One who holds the universe together, preserving its unity, order, and integrity. He performed this divine responsibility while hanging on the cross, and now He performs it from the very center of disorder and chaos, from the realm of death, from the tomb. When He became human, His divinity did not relinquish this cosmic responsibility; otherwise the whole universe would have collapsed. Now He has gone into the very realm of chaos and disorder to vanquish death in order to restore wholeness to His creation. This is indispensable in order for Him to continue to hold the universe together.

But He is also there to bring death to an end. It is because deity is alive inside the tomb that death will be exterminated. Life is more powerful than death. As a result of the presence of God in the sphere of death, something glorious will happen: "He [God] will swallow up [Heb. *billa'*, "swallow, destroy"] death for all time

---

[5] Ellen G. White Comments, in *The Seventh-day Adventist Bible Commentary*, Vol. 5 (Washington, DC: Review and Herald, 1956), 1114.

[forever]" (Isa 25:8). In the tomb we see the Living God destroying death forever by taking it upon Himself.

THE GATE OF LIFE: A CORPSE

I left for last the first thing we would have seen inside the tomb, namely, the corpse of Jesus. This is not just any corpse. In fact, it is a corpse out of place, because He should never have been there. This was the place for sinners, and He was not a sinner. Yet, He is there inside the tomb, dead—eternally dead. He was not pretending to be dead; He was absolutely dead! The corpse is there because it is the corpse of fallen humanity. On the cross the fallen Adamic humanity was executed—He died for all of us, for all humans. The natural human life coming from Adam ended. And those who choose to remain connected to Adam will die, because "in Adam all die," Paul says (1 Cor 15:22). Yet, there is no reason for anyone to die.

This corpse is there because death is the most important biblical symbol of total separation from God. The tomb itself is the space farthest away from God in the cosmos. One descends there in contrast to ascending to "heaven," the space where God is (Isa 7:11; Matt 11:23). John refers to this sphere of death as "a bottomless pit" (Gr. *abussos*, "the abyss; the underworld").

From Friday to Sunday Jesus is there. In this prison house, the human nature is dead, but the divine is alive. What was prefigured in the sanctuary services has become a reality in the person of the Incarnate God. The indestructible life of God has come into direct contact with the uncleanness of death, touching each other because the two natures remained inseparable even in the tomb. The result of the contact is a new life.

The mysterious union of the human and the divine within the tomb radically changes the nature of the tomb. It will no longer be a door leading into the realm of death but the door that will free the captives from the prison of death. And the first one to come out through that door will be the Son of God. This tomb that we are visiting will become the only, exclusive way out of the realm of death, leading us into the divine kingdom of light. Through the imperishable life of the Son of God it would become something similar to a womb. It is like a womb because as a result of the presence of the Incarnate God in it, a new creation will come into existence.

We contemplate what took place inside the tomb that Sunday morning, but we do not fully understand it. In fact, we do not know what happened inside it. We see God and the dust from earth in the form of a lifeless human being. God is not holding the dust of the earth in His hands; He incarnated Himself in living dust, but now this is dead dust. Since the two natures remain united in the tomb, He is incarnated in dead dust. What happened inside the tomb? I can only use Genesis 2 to imagine what may have happened in the tomb.

I would suggest to you that on Sunday morning, at the time appointed by the Lord, the God of life, in the second person of the Godhead, as Creator, infused or breathed a new life into the human nature of Jesus, bringing into existence right there in the tomb a new creation that is not connected at all to the perishable life of Adam. This life breaks forth from the womb through the power of deity. Eternal life was again at the disposal of the human race. "He suffered the death which was ours, that we might receive the life which was His."[6] There is a new creation: "Therefore if anyone is in Christ, he is a new creature [creation]; the old things passed away; behold, new things have come" (2 Cor 5:17). He is a new creation, and if we are incorporated into Him, we are a new creation.

Now from the tomb a new source of life will be available to us: "'For the first man, Adam, became a living soul [person].' The last Adam became a live-giving spirit" (1 Cor 15:45; see Col 3:4). "In Joseph's tomb He wrapped Himself in the garment of immortality, and then waited in the world for a sufficient length of time to put beyond doubt the evidence that He was indeed risen from the dead."[7] The new fountain of life for human beings is the life of the resurrected Lord. "As a member of the human family, He was mortal; but as God, He was the fountain of life to the world."[8]

---

[6] White, *The Desire of Ages*, 25.

[7] Ellen G. White, *Christ Triumphant* (Hagerstown, MD: Review and Herald, 1999), 293.

[8] Ellen G. White, *The Bible Echo*, September 15, 1892, par. 6.

In order for us to be part of the new creation, the work of God in the tomb, we also have to die and go inside the tomb of Jesus. The old person has to die. Have you visited the tomb of Jesus? Yes, you have. We participate in the experience of Jesus through baptism. By faith we die with Him, go into the tomb that is now open to all sinners, and through the power of the new life that we have in Christ, we come back to a new life. It is indeed a new life because it is ours through Christ and not through Adam. It is a new life because it is not under the lordship of sin but under the Lordship of Christ. The tomb of Jesus is empty, and so will also be our tombs.

CONCLUSION

We visited Christ's tomb, and we have chosen to identify ourselves with His experience. Our reflections on what happened inside the tomb should lead us to praise God for what He was willing to do for us, small creatures living on a very small planet in a huge galaxy in a cosmos of inconceivable dimensions. No one will be saved without visiting the tomb of Christ. This is the good news of the gospel. We have been there through baptism, and as a result, we live a new life flowing from the cross of Jesus. We should take every opportunity to invite relatives, friends, and anyone we encounter in our pilgrimage to visit the tomb of Jesus.

CHAPTER 14

"WHAT THINGS?"

Kleber D. Gonçalves

> *Now that same day two of them were going to a village called Emmaus, about seven miles from Jerusalem. They were talking with each other about everything that had happened. As they talked and discussed these things with each other, Jesus himself came up and walked along with them; but they were kept from recognizing him. He asked them, 'What are you discussing together as you walk along?' They stood still, their faces downcast. One of them, named Cleopas, asked him, 'Are you the only one visiting Jerusalem who does not know the things that have happened there in these days?' 'What things?' he asked. (Luke 24:13-19, emphasis added).*[1]

"What things?" That's the question Jesus asked those disciples who were totally disillusioned and disheartened as they were going back home to the small village of Emmaus.

What *things?* Actually, *things* happen. This is part of life in a world spotted by sin. I'm sure all of us agree with that. Different situations come and go. *Things*, in fact, happen. Many times, they happen in a way we simply don't expect.

It's been more than eight months[2] that we have been in this unbelievable and surreal experience facing shutdowns, stay-at-home orders, economic meltdown (the list is long!) due to the worldwide COVID-19 pandemic. A few months ago, we *thought* we would begin to see the flattening of the COVID-19 curve. But

---

[1] Unless otherwise noted, Scripture quotations are from the New International Version.

[2] This message was updated on Nov 11, 2020, to present the current situation of the COVID-19 pandemic in the USA.

suddenly, everything changed. As I write this, we are now facing the worst situation so far. Yesterday, approximately 140,000 new cases were confirmed in the USA. How hard it is to be originally from Brazil but now living in the United States—two nations competing for positions in the top three spots on the list of cases and deaths. How sad! We simply don't know what will come next.

Different situations (good and bad) come and go. As I just said, *things* happen. And not only in the world arena. Things happen to us as well. All of us have gone through moments of deep sadness, or maybe pain, perhaps deception. Moments like these come to us— moments in which we feel that our dreams have been destroyed.

Actually, depending on your age, it does not need to be something *that* important to make you feel this way. Do you remember that Christmas night "tragedy" when you were waiting for a bicycle, but instead, you got a pair of socks? Yes, I *do* remember that! We simply didn't get what we wanted!

As we get older, there are many other things that *happen* that bring the same result in us:

- The friend that no longer remembers.

- The spouse that no longer fulfills the promise.

- The criticism that has no reason.

- The trust that is not reciprocated.

- The pain that is totally unexpected.

- The separation that hurts us so deeply.

Losses in life. With the current pandemic, some of us are now seeing people close to us die. They are not simple numbers. They are not a statistic anymore. They are people we know. And every time we face situations like these, we have to make a decision: what do we do when our heart is broken? How do we deal with disappointment, pain, sorrow?

That's exactly what we find in the well-known story record- ed in Luke 24. Those two followers of Christ had their hearts broken with everything that had happened in the past couple of days. Their world had collapsed. A deep and indescribable sorrow took over their hearts.

ON THE WAY TO EMMAUS

We can easily picture the situation and how they were feeling. Their thoughts were occupied by sadness, deception, and doubt. **"They were talking with each other about everything that had happened"** (Luke 24:14). It is not hard to imagine what was going through the minds of these two men. Maybe they were asking things like these:

- "Why have the people rejected Jesus this way?" "Why did they kill Him with such brutality?"

- "He could have come down from the cross. Why didn't He use His power to do so?"

- "Pilate did what he wanted. The disciples didn't do anything."

- "What about our dream? What about us?! What are we going to do now?"

Usually, in moments like these we have a lot of questions but very few answers. But as these two were walking, a Stranger came closer and joined them in their journey, "but [amazingly!] **they were kept from recognizing him**" (Luke 24:16). Jesus was now with them, but they simply could not see. They didn't recognize the Master.

How come?

Sadness can do that to us. Deception can block our minds. Pain can harden our hearts. Doubt can blind our eyes—even in the presence of God. And right here there is a tremendous lesson for all of us: if we lose hope, despair can darken our vision.

I'm sure you remember the amazing story of Jacob when he was fleeing from his brother and had the stairway dream experience. Do you remember what he said after he woke up? In the book of Genesis, we read: **"When Jacob awoke from his sleep, he thought, 'Surely the Lord is in this place, *and I was not aware of it*'"** (Gen 28:16, emphasis added).

Did you notice what Jacob said? "The Lord is in this place, and I was *not* aware of it." This was exactly what happened to Cleopas and his friend. They could not see. They could not believe. They even mentioned to Jesus what they heard from the women who went to the tomb earlier that same day.

It is not hard to imagine how they were describing "the things" to Jesus. Most probably, their voices, their attitude, their body language—everything was so negative.

"As if His death were not enough, now they are saying that His body was stolen, and some of our friends now are even thinking He has been resurrected."

Maybe they even asked, looking at Jesus:

"Can *You* believe it?!"

They couldn't. *No way!!* They were not going to be "deceived" this time. Once was enough. They would not expose themselves to the mockery again. They would not allow their hearts to be captivated by another dream. Nope. Not again.

But let me ask you something: can we blame them for having this kind of attitude?

Usually, when we are rejected, we don't go back for more. When we are criticized, we don't risk anymore. When we are ignored, we don't try again. When we are misled, we don't trust. When we are attacked, we don't forgive. That's the human heart. That's the "normal" human nature. And probably it will get even worse in the "new normal," post-pandemic world ahead of us!

But this is dangerous business. Why? Because if we lose hope, we run the risk of crossing the line, of passing the limit. What limit? The limit between disappointment and anger. The limit between sadness and guilt. The limit between pain and hate.

This is what happens with those who lose hope. However, in moments when "things happen," we need to keep our eyes focused on what really matters. We need to look forward. We need to listen and allow the Holy Spirit to do with us what the Master did with Cleopas and his companion on their way to Emmaus.

THE ENCOUNTER WITH JESUS

First of all, we can never ever forget that Jesus came to them in the very moment they needed Him the most: **"Jesus himself came up and walked along with them"** (Luke 24:15). Christ came to them in the midst of their greatest pain and doubt!

Jesus embraced them in the moment when their hope was basically gone. They said to Jesus: **"'We *had hoped* that he was the one who was going to redeem Israel'"** (Luke 24:21, emphasis added).

They had hoped

that Jesus would remove Herod from his throne;

that Jesus would expel the Romans;

that Jesus would reign in Israel;

that Jesus would not allow Himself to be arrested;

that He would come down from the cross;

that Jesus would be the fulfillment of their dreams.

But Jesus didn't do what they had hoped. Jesus didn't do what they wanted.

By the way, what do *you* want? What do I want? Peace? Freedom? A world without problems? A world without tragedies? The same church we had before?

We must never forget that *Jesus didn't do what they wanted, but He did what they really needed!* Many times, we don't understand what goes on around us. As Paul says:

Now we see things imperfectly, like puzzling reflections in a mirror, but then we will see everything with perfect clarity. All that I know now is partial and incomplete, but then I will know everything completely, just as God now knows me completely (1 Cor 13:12, NLT).

When "things happen," we usually have more questions than answers. But these are moments in which we need to remind ourselves in Whom we have believed.

Those two disciples wanted to see the redemption of Israel as a nation, but God wanted something bigger. He chose to fight the battle they would never be able to win—the battle none of us would ever be able to succeed in.

God said *No* to what the disciples wanted, and *Yes* to what they—without knowing—needed the most.

Friends, it is always good to remember that God is willing to give us not what we want, but what we really need. We need hope, even in the midst of crisis, confusion, and tribulation. We need optimism, even when we have to face challenges. We need faith, even in the midst of doubt.

How is it possible to have these things? Simple. We just need to remember what Jesus did with those two disciples as they walked to Emmaus. He told them a story.

CONCLUSION

Do you remember what happened? **"And beginning with Moses and all the Prophets, [*Jesus*]** *explained to them what was said in all the Scriptures concerning himself"* (Luke 24:27, emphasis added).

Jesus told them a story: His story, the story of God's mission in human history. That is the solution for any broken heart: the *same* story. Actually, that's our mission today: in order to "Reach the World," we must share the same story, the full story, the story of the risen Savior—who will soon come back to take us home!

Cleopas and his friend heard what all of us need to hear when we face moments of sadness or pain. Those two disciples heard what we need to share with the whole world. They heard what the whole Scriptures—from Genesis to Revelation—say about Jesus.

We need to hear once again that God is in command. He is the One who will give the last word. We need always to remember that when we face unexpected situations, we don't need to despair.

On the contrary, we can move forward with greater faith, trusting in God's guidance in our lives.

How? Remember and share the story. Are you tired? Remember and share the story. Concerned? Remember and share the story. If you are confused, remember and share the story. Sad? Remember—and share the story!

And never, ever forget: Things happen.

"'What things?' he asked" (Luke 24:19a).

It doesn't matter!

Only *remember* and *share the story.*

CHAPTER 15

THE CHURCH IN THE CONTEMPORARY WORLD

Alberto R. Timm

One of the most amazing natural phenomena in the Amazon region is the so-called "Meeting of the Waters" or "Encounter of the Waters" of the dark Negro River with the muddy Solimões (or Amazon) River. The two rivers run side by side, without mixing, for some 6 km, providing an unforgettable spectacle. The phenomenon occurs due to the differencein density, speed, and temperatures between the two rivers The Solimões River carries many sediments, and it flows up to 6 km/h at a temperature of 22° C.[1] The Negro River has some organic components and flows at about 2 km/h at a temperature of 28° C. But after running side by side for that distance, the waters of the two rivers finally mix together into the huge Lower Amazon River, losing their own peculiarities.

A similar phenomenon occurs also in the religious realm, for time tends to merge religion with the predominant culture.

Sociological studies of religion have shown that religious movements arise normally with the purpose of reforming the culture in which they exist. But in the second century of their existence, after the pioneers and those who knew them passed away, these very same movements tend to lose their identity and to be reabsorbed by the culture they originally intended to reform.[2]

---

[1] Information available at https://www.sciencealert.com/what-causes-brazils-meeting-of-the-waters (accessed February 26, 2020).

[2] Alberto R. Timm, "Podemos ainda ser considerados o 'povo da Bíblia'?" *Revista Adventista*

The process of losing identity is well illustrated in 1 Samuel 8, especially in the arguments used by the Israelites for choosing a king to replace the prophet Samuel. In 1 Samuel 8:1-5 we read,

> Now it came to pass when Samuel was old that he made his sons judges over Israel. The name of his firstborn was Joel, and the name of his second, Abijah; they were judges in Beersheba. But his sons did not walk in his ways; they turned aside after dishonest gain, took bribes, and perverted justice.[3]

> Then all the elders of Israel gathered together and came to Samuel at Ramah, and said to him, "Look, you are old, and your sons do not walk in your ways. Now make us a king to judge us like all the nations."

Some expressions used by the elders of Israel in their dialogue with Samuel are very enlightening for us who live in the 21st century of the Christian era.

"LOOK, YOU ARE OLD"

The story of Samuel is very beautiful and inspiring (see 1 Sam 1-3). Hannah had been barren but, in answer to her prayers, God gave her a son, Samuel, who was dedicated to the Lord even before he was born. Later, when he was still a boy, she took him to the House of the Lord, in Shiloh, to be an assistant to the priest Eli. In reality, God called young Samuel to the prophetic office.

Samuel was loyal to God throughout his life and had a positive influence on the lives of the people of Israel. It is interesting to note that, after his death, "the Israelites gathered together and lamented for him" (1 Sam 25:1). Later, the apostate king Saul even asked a medium at En Dor to "'bring up'" for him, in a séance, the late prophet Samuel (1 Sam 28). Such later incidents reveal the respect and consideration that the nation of Israel had for Samuel.

But at a certain point, when Samuel was already old, the leaders of Israel approached him and said to him: "Look, you are

---

(Brazil), June 2001, 14.

[3] All Bible references are from the New King James Version.

old." This statement did not carry the positive meaning it does in some Asian cultures in which the older someone becomes, the more seriously he or she is taken. The statement had the negative connotation of needing to be replaced. The leaders were actually saying, "You might still be in good health, but we want to replace you. We want 'new blood,' actually a more dynamic and impressive leadership style."

Even leaving out this negative connotation, we have to recognize that our present life is indeed on an unbreakable trajectory. Many products carry on their labels such expressions as "best before," "use by," "sell by," or "expires on." For some products the expiration date is shorter than for others. At any rate, we as human beings also have an expiration date that derives either from our natural aging process, or from our own personal decisions, or even from others who attribute it to us.

In the case of Samuel, the elders of Israel simply imposed it on him. Forgetting that the prophetic office was not a human choice but rather a divine call, those elders believed that the time for the prophet Samuel to be replaced had come and that he himself should choose his own successor to lead God's people.

"AND YOUR SONS DO NOT WALK IN YOUR WAYS"

The most natural option of successor at that time would be one of Samuel's own children; and, for him, the matter had already been settled when he made "his sons judges over Israel" (1 Sam 8:1). But, unfortunately, the children did not have the same integrity as their father. According to the biblical account, "But his sons did not walk in his ways; they turned aside after dishonest gain, took bribes, and perverted justice" (1 Sam 8:3). We are also told that Samuel "had been to some extent too indulgent with his sons, and the result was apparent in their character and life." But "the cases of abuse among the people had not been referred to Samuel."[4] Even so, his heart must have broken when Israel's leaders spoke frankly to him about the problem concerning his sons. They said to him plainly: "'Your sons do not walk in your ways'" (1 Sam 8:5). The accusation in itself was very traumatic,

---

[4] Ellen G. White, *Patriarchs and Prophets* (Washington, DC: Review and Herald, 1890), 604.

but it became almost unbearable because it was undeniable. As often stated, "Against facts, there are no arguments!"

I know many families whose homes used to be "a little heaven on earth,"[5] where parents and children happily shared the same faith and the same spiritual values. But after going to the academy and college the children simply abandoned their parents' faith, moral values, and even lifestyle. Heartbroken, the parents pray incessantly for the reconversion of their children. In the mind of the parents, the same questions keep echoing: "Where did we go wrong? What could we have done differently?"

As a church, we should ask ourselves, "What is the profile of new generations of Adventists? Do they have the same commitment that our pioneers had to the Adventist doctrines and lifestyle? Do we have to admit, like Samuel, that our children 'do not walk' in our ways?" And more, "What are we doing to pass on to them the biblical values of our Adventist heritage?"

"NOW MAKE US A KING TO JUDGE US LIKE ALL THE NATIONS"

In 1 Samuel 8:5, three main reasons are mentioned for choosing a king: (1) "'Look, you are old,'" (2) "'and your sons do not walk in your ways,'" and (3) "'now make us a king to judge us like all the nations.'" The first two reasons were true and irrefutable; but the third reason reveals an almost inevitable trend—the acculturation of faith and the loss of confessional identity under the persistent and convincing appeals of the culture in which we live. Crucial in the passage under consideration is the expression "like all the nations"!

LeRoy E. Froom gets to the heart of the matter by stating that "while the church is evangelizing the world, the world is secularizing the church."[6] Jack Ellul, in his book *The Subversion of Christianity*, asks: How has it come about that the development of Christianity and the church has given birth to a society, a

---

[5] Ellen G. White, *Testimonies for the Church*, vol. 3 (Mountain View, CA: Pacific Press, 1875), 539.

[6] LeRoy E. Froom, *The Coming of the Comforter*, rev. ed. (Washington, DC: Review and Herald, 1949), 131.

civilization, a culture that are completely opposite to what we read in the Bible, to what is indisputably the text of the law, the prophets, Jesus, and Paul?" And the same author adds that "revelation has been progressively modeled and reinterpreted according to the practice of Christianity and the church."[7] It seems that, more and more, "God has been remade in our image and likeness."[8]

This leads us to ask, "Is it possible that Christianity is already in a post-Christian perod? And that Adventism itself is already in a post-Adventist period?" I do not believe that we are living in a post-Christianity and post-Adventism era. The Seventh-day Adventist Church has well-grounded biblical doctrines and well-defined biblical principles. The problem is not with the doctrines and principles themselves, but rather with our lack of personal commitment to those doctrines and principles.

The only way to preserve our denominational identity is to cling unconditionally to the prophetic word like Jehoshaphat, king of Judah, did in his dialogue with Ahab, king of Israel (see 2 Chr 18). The culture of the time was one of absolute secularization and apostasy, but Jehoshaphat had the courage to inquire about "'the word of the Lord,'" even in the face of the presence of Ahab's four hundred false prophets. Jehoshaphat was incisive in his statements: "'Please inquire for the word of the Lord today'" (2 Chr 18:4). "'Is there not still a prophet of the Lord here, that we may inquire of Him?'" (2 Chr 18:6). "'Believe in the Lord your God, and you shall be established; believe His prophets, and you shall prosper'" (2 Chr 20:20).

Faithfulness to the prophetic word means (1) to accept "every word that proceeds from the mouth of God" (Matt 4:4); and (2) to live by what that Word actually says, not what we would like it to say. In other words, the universal principles from God's revelation must be above our personal tastes and preferences. Christconcludes the famous Sermon on the Mount with an analogy of the two foundations and the houses built on them (see Matt 7:24-27). He had previously said: "'Not everyone who says

---

[7] Jack Ellul, *The Subversion of Christianity* (Grand Rapids, MI: Eerdmans, 1986), 3.

[8] Douglas S. Huffman and Eric L. Johnson, eds., *God under Fire* (Grand Rapids, MI: Zondervan, 2002), back cover.

to Me, "Lord, Lord," shall enter the kingdom of heaven, but he who does the will of My Father in heaven"" (Matt 7:21). And in the very analogy of the fundamentals, the foundations, He stresses again the importance of personal commitment to His word (see Matt 7:24-27).

CONCLUSION

One of the most well-known medieval architectural works is the Tower of Pisa in Italy, which has become world famous for its pronounced tilt. The foundation of the tower began to be built in August 1173, but the tower itself, as we know it today, was only completed about 200 years later, due to several interruptions. It has seven regular floors and an eighth floor with a smaller circumference, which houses a steeple with several bells. With a height of almost 60 meters (183 feet) from the bottom to the top, it weighs approximately 14,500 tons. The tower was built on unstable terrain, basically composed of soft claywith some intermediate layers of sand. During construction, the land began to give way. The current slope is now more than five meters (16 feet) off perpendicular.[9] Many efforts have been made to prevent the tower from falling over.

As the Leaning Tower of Pisa is in danger of toppling because it was built on clayey terrain, the spiritual life of many professing Christians may also collapse under the impact of the ideological storms of the last days. Such ruin is usually preceded by (1) a posture of considering the prophetic teachings and values as already obsolete; (2) failing to transmit them to the new generations; and (3) replacing them by the antibiblical components of the predominant culture.

But if we are to maintain our biblical-prophetic identity, we must overcome the cultural temptations that have eroded the identity of many other Christian denominations. We need to ground our lives on the immovable foundation of the Word of God. According to Isaiah 40:8, "The grass withers, the flower fades, but the word of our God stands forever."

---

[9] See "Leaning Tower of Pisa," http://www.towerofpisa.org/leaning-tower-of-pisa-facts/ (accessed February 26, 2020).

CHAPTER 16

THE MISSION OF CHRIST: THE GOSPEL IN THE REAL WORLD[1]

Rick McEdward

Incarnating the gospel into culture demands the very best in our lives. In order to be effective in sharing the gospel, we need to be cautious not to impose too much of our cultural background and make our package of Christianity into a set of externals rather than a change of heart that includes understanding of the Bible, an acceptance of core beliefs, and a change in lifestyle.

As each Adventist is called to bear witness for Christ, we are confronted with circumstances and ways of life that create barriers to understanding. Sometimes we can create new barriers by delivering the good news in ways that are misunderstood.

In this devotional article, I attempt to unpack some of the attitudes that can be included in our mission. We need to find ways of understanding and keys for connecting with people as Jesus did. Then we can be more incarnational with His message to our communities.

In 2001 our family was requested to move as missionaries to Sri Lanka. Our preparation for mission included language study. As we prepared for mission service, we knew our lives were about to take a dramatic turn. Our dreams of sharing the gospel with Buddhists, Hindus, and Muslims were soon to become a reality. I imagined learning the language, telling people stories of Jesus,

---

[1] Test originally published in Gregory Whitsett and Amy Whitsett, eds., *Winning Hearts: Leading Buddhists to Faith in God* (Silver Spring, MD: General Conference of Seventh-day Adventists, 2016), 29-38. Used by permission.

and inviting people to follow Him. Our hearts were burning with anticipation leading up to our departure.

We drove along the streets at 3:30 a.m. to our new home, passing Buddha statues on every corner, where people lit lamps and offered sacrifices. We noticed Bo trees, held in sacred honor, which had prayer flags tied around them. Over the first few months we had such a feeling of chaos, change, and confusion about everything we were experiencing. We wondered how we would ever make a difference for the people all around us, how could we bring the gospel to our community and to the nation.

Each morning I woke up before dawn to the chanting of the Pirith Potak, the book of protection, from the Buddhist Temple just down the dusty road from our home. Devotees, even at this early hour, were up praying, offering sacrifices, and chanting the Dhamapada. Buddhist and Hindu festivals were frequent, bringing a new pace to life in our new home.

It was then that I really began to wonder, what is it that Jesus has called me here for? What is the mission of Christ for me in Sri Lanka? With all I see around me, how will Jesus live out His mission in me? If our time in Sri Lanka was to be of any benefit at all, I wanted Christ to be the Lord of our mission. We pled with God for answers on how to live and how to go about His work.

So today I want to share with you some key aspects to the mission of Christ in the real world. In order to do this, I want to spend some time digging deeper in the beginning of the New Testament, in the book of Matthew. So, for a few moments, let's look at His mission as it is recorded in Scripture.

THE LINEAGE OF CHRIST

Matthew chapter 1 gives us a special glimpse into the mind of the Jew of the 1st Century. Lineage was important, as it gave you a place in society, a family to belong to, and an ancestral land given to you by God when the land was divided by Moses.

IT ENCAPSULATED ALL OF THE HISTORY OF ISRAEL
From the calling of Abraham until the birth of Christ, the genealogy given in Matthew 1 feels like a who's who of the history of the nation. Patriarchs are included, the lineage of David is

included, and several kings are included. It covers the three key epochs of Israel's history up to that point: Patriarchs, Monarchy, and Exile.

BOTH COVENANTS ARE INCLUDED

The Abrahamic and the Davidic covenants are included in this passage. With the inclusion of the exile, Israel's unfaithfulness to both of these covenants is also included. This unique feature of Christ's lineage in Matthew 1 is fascinating in that it brings the two covenants into one family line, making this lineage special. It brings a focus to the story Matthew is presenting from the start, by reiterating the credentials of the person the story is about.

THERE ARE SOME INTERESTING NUMBERS IN THE STORY

While issues regarding math are strongly suspect for biblical interpretation, there is mention here of the fourteen generations from Abraham to David, fourteen from David to the Exile, and fourteen from the Exile to Christ.

THERE ARE IDIOSYNCRASIES IN THE MATTHEW LINEAGE

There are four women included in this lineage besides Mary: Tamar, Rahab, Ruth, and Bathsheba. All of these women are known to the readers from the Old Testament; this list includes two prostitutes, one Moabitess, and one likely a Hittite. All of them knew more than one man. It is reasonable to ask why these women are included. Could it be that the author mentions these women to support Mary who was pregnant while still betrothed to Joseph? Could it be that the inclusion of non-Israelites can support the universalization of the Covenant toward those not of Jewish descent? Could it be that the lineage of Christ could include those with a fallen past, who have become attached to Christ?

The lineage mentioned by Matthew is Joseph's family, who in practical terms had little to do with the birth of Christ, except as he served as an escort and husband to Mary. Joseph's lineage, it could be claimed, is not the lineage of Christ at all.

LINEAGE IN THE MEANING OF CHRIST

In the Matthew lineage the author is calling out that at His birth, Christ takes onto himself in bodily form the entire history of Israel—its failures and accomplishments, its identity and separation from God. Step by step Christ walks over Israel's history, but He does so without falling. Jesus becomes the "prophet like unto Moses" (see Deut 18:15) and the new lawgiver in the Sermon on the Mount. Jesus survives the murderous intentions of a king at birth and is sheltered in Egypt. Jesus is baptized in the Jordan, as Moses had been given new life in the River Nile. Jesus survives 40 days in the wilderness as Israel survived 40 years. Jesus embodies each part of the sanctuary service, illustrating that the panorama of salvation pictured in the tabernacle and temple are also embodied in the great controversy seen in Christ's life, zdeath, and resurrection. Jesus' name is the Greek form of Joshua, which in its essence means deliverer or salvation.

The history of Israel is seen as being fulfilled in Christ in the following ways:[2]

- Jesus becomes the new David with the triumphant entrance into Jerusalem.

- Jesus becomes the new Solomon with wisdom, parables, and proverbs.

- Jesus becomes the new Elijah and Elisha with healing, miracles, and confronting of leaders.

- Jesus becomes the Old Testament Jacob, with 12 disciples replacing the 12 patriarchs.

- Jesus takes the place of the Old Testament prophets with His woes to the Pharisees.

Jesus relives the history of Israel. The loving God of the covenant is included here, the years of slavery and God's redemption, the failures in the wilderness, the establishment of the sacrificial system, the giving of the law, the lostness of the era of the judges, the glory of the Kingdom under David and Solomon, the dark ages of Israel's history with evil kings and a divided kingdom. "He did **evil** in the eyes of the LORD, following the ways of his father and committing the same sin his father had caused Israel to commit"

---

[2] Some of these points were covered in and inspired by the class "Salvation" taught by Jon Paulien, Andrews University, 1990.

(1 Kings 15:26[3] and other similar passages, emphasis added) seemed like a repeated theme of the era. Even the quiet era of the intertestamental time, during which there was a conspicuous lack of prophets as spokesmen for God, is included in Matthew's lineage.

THE MESSIAH

Suddenly, as if bursting on the scene of the Roman-occupied territories, is the baby, born to Mary, who was engaged to be married. Joseph's righteous plan to break the engagement quietly so as not to cause her public disgrace was rebuked by an angel of God. Through this story, in Joseph and Mary, we meet the first two individuals who begin to catch a glimpse of the mystery of the incarnation. "She will give birth to a son, and you are to give him the name Jesus, because he will save his people from their sins" (Matt 1:21).

His name is Jesus. With words so profound yet so mysterious, the announcement is made—"'and they will call him Immanuel' (which means, 'God with us')" (Matt 1:23b).

The mystery of the incarnation cannot be overestimated. While each of the four Gospels provides us a special view of the ultimate act in history, the perspective that each of them provides is unique. It is as if four authors were trying to describe the beauty beneath the oceans, the lush jungles of the tropics with their flora and fauna, and the majestic glacial peaks of the Andean mountains—all at once. Each Gospel writer gives us beauty, delicacy, artistry, and grandeur in his pictures of Christ's mission.

At the time of Christ's birth there was a tremendous sense of expectancy. Messianic groups had formed to proclaim the time of arrival. The knowledge of Daniel's prophecy was not lost, affirming the arrival time of the new king. Prophecy was expected to be fulfilled; a deliverer would come and free Israel from the Romans. Jesus came at a time when the Jews anticipated a political liberator. But first-century Jews did not get what they expected.

---

[3] Unless otherwise noted, Bible passages are quoted from the New International Version.

What they actually saw was a picture of God so different from anything they had imagined. Due to this radical change, they did not recognize the Messiah when He came.

THE INCARNATION AND MISSION

I want to bring into focus eight essential characteristics of the Incarnation that provide us with a radical foundation for mission. These eight aspects of the incarnation are not meant to represent a complete picture, for that would ruin the sense of mystery that necessarily surrounds divinity in human flesh.

GOD CAME DOWN

God condescended to be with us. He became a human. In so doing, Jesus presents a different picture of God, a God who is interested in us, a God whose love is so intent on being with His creation that He longed to be with us. Prior to the fall at the beginning of human history, God had fellowshipped personally with His creation. After the fall, the direct interaction of God with man was seen at key moments—God interacted through providence and revelation, but rarely face to face. The Sanctuary was provided as a picture of God's love and the plan of salvation, but this was an inadequate substitute. For the bulk of human history, until the appearance of Christ, God had desired fellowship with people. In the incarnation we see part of the motive of God in the words, "God with us."

John 1 gives us the idea that God came in human flesh in Jesus Christ and became "the word," the "logos." As God spoke the world into existence through Jesus, now God's word becomes alive in Jesus.

HE MADE HIMSELF NOTHING

Philippians 2 is a key text for understanding the incarnation. Verses 6 and 7 read:

> Who, being in very nature God, did not consider equality with God something to be used to his own advantage;
>
> rather, he made himself nothing by taking the very nature of a servant, being made in human likeness.

God subjected Himself not only to be a human, but also to be born in poverty, to take on the role of a servant. He made Himself nothing for us, as Mark 10:45 recorded in His own words: "For even the Son of Man did not come to be served, but to serve, and to give his life as a ransom for many."

Jesus came by surprise, in part because though the expectation was rife that he would come as a conqueror, he came instead as a servant. This significant departure from the type of messiah that people were anticipating marked Jesus' ministry for rejection by many.

HE IDENTIFIED WITH US

Jesus lived everyday life as a person and lived it with every limitation we have today. He experienced grief and joy, knew hunger and sleeplessness, experienced friendship and rejection. Christ had to get dressed, take baths, and deal with cuts and bruises as we do today. It is likely that Palestine had mosquitos, flies, and roaches; Jesus had to deal with the everyday realities of life.

Jesus met people where they were. He practiced the discipline of giving messages based on the hearers' readiness to receive, rather than giving everything in statements of propositional truth. Jesus wanted His message to have the best chance of reception, so He spoke from everyday experience and used language that was common to the people around Him.

HE CAME AS A BABY

Jesus came into humanity as a learner, not an expert. Christ was the ultimate person and the divine-human combination. If ever there was a rationale for someone to present himself as having all of life's pieces in proper order, Jesus surely had it. Yet Jesus chose to come as an infant and experience childhood and grow into adulthood. He did not have to be a learner, but He carefully humbled Himself from the standpoint of heaven in order to be relevant to a world that was not ready to receive Him.

HE TOOK ON THE CULTURE OF THE PEOPLE HE WAS TRYING TO REACH

Jesus was born in a Jewish home; He went through Jewish rites of passage. In growing up He learned the ways of life and practiced the culture of His Jewish ancestry. He extended Himself to learn an earthly culture in order to reveal God's love to those whom God had chosen to receive the revelation of God in the flesh.

HE TOUCHED THEM IN THEIR NEEDS, MEETING THEIR PHYSICAL NEEDS BEFORE THEIR SPIRITUAL ONES

An incarnational presence would not be complete without the real needs of people. Jesus understood their hunger and thirst. He ministered to their diseases and at the same time was not contaminated by them. In Matthew 8 and 9, Jesus heals over and over again. He touches people, casts out demons, and performs miracles. Jesus displayed compassion for people at the level of their physical pain.

> Christ's method alone will give true success in reaching the people. The Savior mingled with men as one who desired their good. He showed His sympathy for them, ministered to their needs, and won their confidence. Then He bade them, "Follow Me."

> There is need of coming close to the people by personal effort. If less time were given to sermonizing, and more time were spent in personal ministry, greater results would be seen. The poor are to be relieved, the sick cared for, the sorrowing and the bereaved comforted, the ignorant instructed, the inexperienced counseled. We are to weep with those that weep, and rejoice with those that rejoice. Accompanied by the power of persuasion, the power of prayer, the power of the love of God, this work will not, cannot, be without fruit.[4]

WHEN HE SPOKE, HE TALKED IN WAYS THEY COULD UNDERSTAND

Jesus told stories, parables, and proverbs. He related to people in ways of familiarity. He told agricultural stories, a topic familiar to them in the first century. He told stories about shepherds, householders, and bosses. Each of the stories Jesus used communicated important truth, but did it in ways people could grasp.

---

[4] Ellen G. White, *The Ministry of Healing* (Mountain View, CA: Pacific Press, 1905), 143-144.

HE CAME TO GIVE HIS LIFE FOR THOSE TO WHOM HE WAS MINISTERING

Jesus did not stop at being born in an uncomfortable situation or providing the daily needs and miracles for people who were sometimes ungrateful. He gave the ultimate gift by giving His life for those He came to serve. Ultimately that means He came to save us, but Jesus saved us with His death.

HIS MISSION AND OURS

With a great passion for humanity, Jesus gave up everything. Consider what Jesus lost in coming to this earth. Think about the heavenly courts, the comforts and peace of dwelling above this earth. The angels in chorus, the beauty and undimmed splendor, the throne of God in all its majesty—these were all part of His routine. He was protected from privations, disease, and the consequences of fallen life here on earth. He had perfect communion with God the Father and the Holy Spirit. He could have the ministry of millions of angels should any need arise in His heavenly ministry. Could Christ, the Son of God, have enacted the crucial phase of the plan of salvation from heaven?

Perhaps, but He did not. He chose to be born as a baby, to a poor family, under questionable circumstances regarding the marriage of his parents. He chose to be born in the non-sterile environment of an animal barn with hay, straw, dung, and flies. The sights, sounds, and smells of real life were all around Him. How uncomfortable an entrance this must have been for the King of the universe!

Raised in a family, learning the language of the people, working in the carpenter shop, perhaps even subject to hitting His thumb with the hammer—Jesus lived a normal boyhood life with the rustle and bustle of the village and the play of boys in the neighborhood.

As an adult after leaving home, He had no job, He never married, and He was homeless. He wandered with His followers from place to place, taking handouts and sometimes staying all night outside under the stars in the countryside of Palestine.

Yet all these disadvantages could not temper His love for us. He literally gave up everything in order to save us. Jesus relinquished Himself to a criminal's death on a device of Roman torture for the two-fold purpose of: a. revealing on a grand scale His love for us; and, b. consummating the plan of salvation that had been in process already for thousands of years.

His mission was selfless, submitted, and serving. He suffered as a human, He was tempted as a human, and He lived without sin or compromise.

What would it be like today if we had two thousand missionaries who went completely with the attitude of Christ, who were not looking for a specific call from the church, but in their commitment to Christ and His church were willing to go without the security of church employment?

How would the effectiveness of our mission change if we took on the mystery of incarnation by coming into cultures as learners, identifying with the people, giving up position and power and wealth, living as the culture dictated but in practical, yet godly, ways, and longing for fellowship with the people we have come to serve?

What impact would it make if we so identified with the people around us that we became participants in the culture rather than pulling away to associate with people like ourselves or finding escape into our own cultural lifestyle that has more abundance and wealth than most of earth's history has known?

Mission is about the heart. We often focus on the surface issues, but the heart remains untouched. When we speak in people's language and culture and present our God in such a way that people get the message, then there is a chance for God to grab the heart. We have sometimes put things in the wrong order—we have aimed to fix the externals first instead of reaching the heart.

AN EXAMPLE OF INCARNATIONAL MISSION

Tim and Wendy are close friends of mine who lived in Cambodia for the past 18 years. When they saved up enough money by working for the church, they quit their good-paying, secure jobs and purchased 19 hectares of land not far from the northern city of Siam Reap. They built a small Cambodian-style wooden home, where they began to raise their family. The area was a rice-growing area, so Tim began by planting rice.

God blessed the decision to purchase this property. What was not obvious at the time of purchase was that this dry piece of land was the exact footprint of the water table. While all of the area residents have struggled with digging wells and hitting dry spots, Wat Preah Yesu has always had an abundant water supply.

Three primary commitments drove the beginnings of Wat Preah Yesu. 1. Tim and Wendy committed totally to living like the people around them. 2. They would never ask for money but would simply pray for God to supply their needs and the needs for the ministry they started; they would only make people aware of how God was blessing their ministry and would leave the rest to God. 3. Their ministry was totally focused on helping Cambodians come to faith in Christ and become powerful witnesses for Him.

Tim and Wendy started off with a small health clinic, using Wendy's background. They also saw a great need for a discipleship-based training center for the nation of Cambodia, where the church was growing following the repatriation of hundreds of thousands of people from refugee camps in Thailand. At the collapse of the Pol Plot era, many who had become Christians as refugees now returned to their country.

As the church grew in numbers, Tim and Wendy saw a great need for giving a stronger biblical and ministry foundation to the new Adventists. They started providing six-month discipleship training programs. During this time of their ministry, spiritually oppressed people repeatedly found relief by the power of God. Tim tells stories of how, over and over again, demonized men and women would find their way, somehow, to Wat Preah Yesu. Some of those who were delivered from evil became faithful Christian witnesses for God's glory.

The local health authorities closed the small medical clinic, so Tim and Wendy turned their focus to starting a school where children of the village could be educated but also could grow in the grace of Christ. Over the years a beautiful school has developed, where more than 300 young people are being discipled in the grace of Christ. They have day students who come each day, but they also have dorms where youth can stay as needed for schooling.

A few years ago, Tim and Wendy felt a strong burden for the children left as orphans because of the spread of AIDS in

Cambodia. In prayer they sought God's help, which He supplied abundantly. They started off with one children's home, operated completely like a very large but normal family with a mom and dad, duties around the house, meals together, and other common family experiences. The homes were set up to do their own cooking, budgeting, and taking care of the children, so that they would feel as much like a normal home as possible. The first home filled up within the first few months. As a result of the tremendous need, Wat Preah Yesu has added homes each year. As of this year there are now nine children's homes opened, with as many as sixteen children in each home.

In 2010, Wat Preah Yesu added one more dimension to sharing Christ with Cambodia by opening a television and radio production studio. The productions are all in the local language, with the aim to share the good news with Cambodia, while training young people to produce family, health, and gospel materials for their country.

Tim and Wendy have given all that the Lord has provided to the Cambodia Adventist Mission and have kept nothing for themselves as they continue to minister for God in Cambodia. In fact, they have been living in the same traditional wooden Cambodian home that has been their base for all these years.

So, what is Christ's mission in the real world?

Hebrews 2:14-17:

Since the children have flesh and blood, he too shared in their humanity so that by his death he might break the power of him who holds the power of death—that is, the devil—and free those who all their lives were held in slavery by their fear of death. For surely it is not angels he helps, but Abraham's descendants. For this reason he had to be made like them, fully human in every way, in order that he might become a merciful and faithful high priest in service to God, and that he might make atonement for the sins of the people.

If we are called to be like Christ, we are called to be in culture, with people, and serving faithfully.

CHAPTER 17

RECLAIM YOUR FIRST LOVE

S. Joseph Kidder

> "'To the angel of the church in Ephesus write:
>
> These are the words of him who holds the seven stars in his right hand and walks among the seven golden lampstands. I know your deeds, your hard work and your perseverance. I know that you cannot tolerate wicked people, that you have tested those who claim to be apostles but are not and have found them false. You have persevered and have endured hardships for my name and have not grown weary.
>
> Yet I hold this against you: You have forsaken the love you had at first. Consider how far you have fallen! Repent and do the things you did at first. If you do not repent, I will come to you and remove your lampstand from its place.'" Revelation 2:1-5[1]

Elementary-aged children were asked what they thought about love. Here are some of their responses:

Glenn, age 7: "If falling in love is anything like learning how to spell, I don't want to do it. It takes too long."

Regina, age 10, agrees: "I'm not rushing into love. I'm finding fourth grade hard enough."

Angie, age 10: "Most men are brainless, so you might have to try more than once to find a live one."

Dave, age 8: "Love will find you, even if you are trying to hide from it. I've been trying to hide from it since I was five, but the girls keep finding me."

---

[1] All Bible quotations are from the NIV unless otherwise stated.

Colin, age 11: "Love is when a boy thinks a girl is pretty."

Reilly, age 12: "Love is just being yourself, but if you are mean, you might have to change."

Amanda, age 12: "I think love is crazy because you have to kiss them over and over."[2]

DEFINITION OF LOVE

Love is a beautiful and mysterious part of our lives. When we are in love, our eyes sparkle, our faces light up, and according to studies, four small sections of our brains are activated in a positive way. Andreas Bartels, a research fellow at University College London, says it is the common denominator of romantic love.[3]

As test subjects were shown photographs of their sweethearts, certain areas of their brains lit up, which means a higher flow of blood went to those parts of the brain. These "love spots" were not the same as sections that become active when someone feels simple lust. In addition, looking at these pictures of their sweethearts also reduced activity in three larger areas that are active when people are upset or depressed.[4] So in our text from Revelation 2, it is as if Jesus is telling them there are certain parts of their brains that do not light up like they used to. But how did that happen? How did they forsake Jesus, their first love?

In the beginning of Revelation 2, Jesus points out to the church at Ephesus that they have forsaken their first love.

Yet I hold this against you: You have forsaken the love you had at first. Consider how far you have fallen! Repent and do the things you did at first. If you do not repent, I will come to you and remove your lampstand from its place (Rev 2:4-5).

---

[2] See https://www.radford.edu/~ibarland/Public/Humor/kidsOnLove (accessed October 11, 2021).

[3] See "The Neural Basis of Romantic Love" by Andreas Bartels and Semir Zeki. http://www.vislab.ucl.ac.uk/pdf/NeuralBasisOfLove.pdf (accessed October 11, 2021).

[4] Ibid.

The Greek word used here is agape love, which is found 116 times in text underlying the *King James Bible*. The meaning of this word is "affection, good will, love, benevolence, brotherly love."[5] This is the highest kind of love. "We love because he first loved us" (1 John 4:19). "This love is characterized by unselfishness and giving, even to the point of sacrifice. It's an unconditional love that doesn't judge based on performance."[6] It is this kind of unconditional love[7] that the members of the Ephesian Church lost, and it is this kind of love that Jesus wants to see in our hearts.

THE CHURCH IN EPHESUS

Ephesus was world-famous as a religious, cultural, and economic center. It had the notable temple of Diana, a fertility goddess worshiped with cultic sexual practices. Her temple was supported by 127 pillars, each pillar sixty feet tall, and it was adorned with great sculptures.[8]

This was the city where Paul established a church and ministered for three years (Acts 19:1-10, Acts 20:31). It was the city where Aquilla and Priscilla ministered along with Apollos (Acts 18:24-28), and where Paul's close associate, Timothy, also ministered (1 Tim 1:3). Ephesus became the residence of the Apostle John before and after his exile. Many believe this church may well represent the apostolic age in its moral and doctrinal purity, but no church stands there today.[9]

---

[5] See https://www.blueletterbible.org/lang/lexicon/lexicon.cfm?Strongs=G26&t=KJV (accessed October 11, 2021).

[6] See https://kenboa.org/living-out-your-faith/five-loves-greatest-agape/ (accessed October 11, 2021).

[7] Kristi Walker, https://www.christianity.com/wiki/christian-terms/what-is-love.html (accessed October 11, 2021).

[8] For further study on Revelation chapter 2, see David Guzik's study guide at https://www.blueletterbible.org/Comm/archives/guzik_david/studyguide_rev/rev_2.cfm (accessed October 11, 2021).

[9] See bible.org's "The Message to Ephesus." https://bible.org/seriespage/message-ephesus-rev-21-7 (accessed October 11, 2021).

I KNOW YOUR WORKS

In the midst of all of this, Jesus sent the Ephesians a three-part letter outlining their good works, what they forsook, and the remedy to restore what was forsaken.

He started by saying, "I know your works." Your works, your labor, your patience—Jesus knows what this church is doing right. They work hard for the Lord, and they have godly endurance.

Below is a list of all the good things they were doing in this church:

- I know your deeds,

- Your hard work [labor, NKJV],

- Your perseverance[10] [patience, NKJV],

- I know that you cannot tolerate wicked people,

- That you have tested those who claim to be apostles but are not, and have found them false.

- You have persevered [this is the second time perseverance is mentioned], and

- Have endured hardships for my name, and

- Have not grown weary.

This was a very busy, active, serving church, with a schedule full of ministries. It was also a *sacrificing* church, for the word *labor* means "toil to the point of exhaustion."[11] The Ephesian Christians paid a price to serve the Lord.

---

[10] Perseverance or patience is the great ancient Greek word *hypomonē*, which means "steadfast endurance." In this sense, the church was rock-solid. https://www.blueletterbible.org/nkjv /rev/2/1/t_conc_1169003 (accessed October 11, 2021).

[11] See Joe Quatrone, Jr's article "Christ and the Churches: Part 1 (Revelation 2:1-11)." https://jo-equatronejr.wordpress.com/2015/05/20/christ-and-the-churches-part-1-revelation-2/ (accessed October 11, 2021).

They were a *steadfast* assembly, for the word *perseverance* carries the meaning of "endurance under trial." They kept going when the going was tough.[12]

The Ephesian church also pursued doctrinal purity. Paul had warned the Ephesians,

> I know that after I leave, savage wolves will come in among you and will not spare the flock. Even from your own number men will arise and distort the truth in order to draw away disciples after them. So be on your guard! Remember that for three years I never stopped warning each of you night and day with tears (Acts 20:29-31).

The church today must also thoroughly test those who claim to be messengers or teachers from God. However, without love, a strong focus on doctrinal purity will make a congregation cold, suspicious, and intolerant.

In summary, the Church of Ephesus persevered with patience and labored for Jesus' sake without becoming weary. They demonstrated a godly perseverance that we should imitate today. By all outward appearances, this was a solid church with sound doctrinal purity and great service and outreach to the community. But there was something extremely important that was gradually disappearing from that church: their first love. "Religion in the church of Ephesus became legalistic and loveless. The vertical relationship with God normally defines the horizontal relationship with humanity."[13] Their first love had left their hearts. Without love, all is in vain.[14]

Oswald Chambers makes it clear that it is easier for Christians to do service than to commit their lives fully to devotion and intimacy with God. He writes,

---

[12] Quatrone, *Christ and the Churches*.

[13] Ranko Stefanovic, *Revelation of Jesus Christ: Commentary on the Book of Revelation*, 2nd ed. (Berrien Springs, MI: Andrews University Press, 2009), 118.

[14] For more details on the Church of Ephesus, see Stefanovic, *Revelation*, 113-121.

Beware of anything that competes with your loyalty to Jesus Christ. The greatest competitor of true devotion to Jesus is the service we do for Him. It is easier to serve than to pour out our lives completely for Him. Are we more devoted to service than we are to Jesus Christ Himself?[15]

FORSAKING YOUR FIRST LOVE

Have you ever seen a man and a woman in love? How often do they get together? They meet whenever and wherever they can! You can hardly separate them. At the beginning of a loving relationship, the man opens the door, pulls out the chair, and they spend hours talking to one another. Why would they do that? Because they are in love. If they stopped getting together whenever they could, they might drift apart, and they do not want that.

If you love Jesus, you will want to spend time with Him. Because you love Him, you will want to make the time. And the result of spending time with Jesus and loving him wholeheartedly is that some radical changes will take place in your life. Here are some biblical examples of what it means to love Jesus.

- To receive him into our hearts (John 1:12-13).

- To treasure Him above all things (Luke 14:26, 16:13).

- To keep His commandments (John 14:15).[16]

- To follow Him wherever He leads (John 10:4).

- To obey Him, whatever He asks (1 John 3:22).

- To trust Him, whatever the trial (1 Peter 1:6-9).

- To reflect the love that God has for us (1 John 4:10).

- To care for the ones He loves (1 John 4:19; see also John 21:16).[17]

---

[15] Oswald Chambers, *My Utmost for His Highest* (Grand Rapids: MI; Discovery House Publishers, 2012), January 18.

[16] See https://www.compellingtruth.org/love-Jesus.html (accessed October 11, 2021).

[17] See https://www.gotquestions.org/love-Jesus.html (accessed October 11, 2021).

All of these commitments come as a result of loving Jesus and spending time with him. People who do not make the time drift away from Him, and they start forsaking their first love. Merriam-Webster defines "forsake" as to renounce or turn away from entirely, to give up or leave (someone or something) entirely. Synonyms include: abandon, desert, leave, maroon, quit, and strand. The opposite of "forsake" is "reclaim." To reclaim something is to restore it to a previous natural state.

The word "forsaken" in Revelation 2:4 is taken from the Greek word *aphiēmi*, which means "to leave, forsake, depart."[18] It stresses a deliberate act for which one is personally responsible. This is not *lost* love that happened by accident, but a *left* love[19] that happened gradually and suggests three particular problems:

- They had moved away from their first love and position of devotion and fervor for the Savior by a gradual departure (Heb. 3:7-8).

- They came to put service for the Lord ahead of love, devotion, and fellowship with Him (1 Thess 1:3; cf. Prov 4:23). Like Martha, we can be so busy working for Christ that we have no time to love Him (Luke 10:38-42).

- Their labor gradually came to be merely mechanical, the thing they were responsible to do, but the Savior wants it to be the result of the abiding life, the result of an intimate walk with Him through the Spirit of God (John 15:1-7; Gal. 5:1-5, 16-26; Eph. 5:18).

SPIRITUAL HEALTH VERSUS SPIRITUAL BUSYNESS

The Church of Ephesus was spiritually busy but not spiritually healthy, because they left their first love. "To the public, the Ephesian church was successful; to Christ, it had fallen."[20] The question for us is, are we spiritually healthy, or are we just spiritually busy?

---

[18] See Blue Letter Bible's definition of "aphiēmi": https://www.blueletterbible.org/lang/lexicon/lexicon.cfm?Strongs=G863&t=NIV (accessed January 29, 2021).

[19] See bible.org's https://bible.org/seriespage/message-ephesus-rev-21-7 (accessed January 29, 2021).

[20] See bible.org's "The Message to Ephesus": https://bible.org/seriespage/3-message-ephesus-rev-21-7 (accessed January 29, 2021).

I experienced this lesson in a personal way some time ago when I was flying from the West Coast back home. I had been the speaker at a camp meeting. My part was on Sabbath, but someone else had spoken at the meeting I attended on Friday night. His topic was the Second Coming of Christ. The sermon was well-crafted and delivered, but I found my mind wandering, not engaged with the speaker. I even thought that if he lost his voice, I could finish the sermon for him because of my familiarity with the subject.

On my flight back home, after preaching, I reflected on the apathy I had experienced. I took my Bible and happened to open it to Revelation chapter 2, the Letter to the Church in Ephesus. As I reflected on the weekend, I felt God convicting me about my disengagement, both to the speaker, and in my faith. This conviction brought me back to the first time I had heard about the Second Coming. It seemed now like the more knowledge I had about the Second Coming, the less fervent anticipation I had for it. Yet Ellen G. White expressed the sentiment that greater knowledge should lead to a greater passion for Jesus Christ.

> The first affection of the convert to Christ is deep, full, and ardent. It is not necessary that this love should become less as knowledge increases, as the more and increased light shines upon him. That love should become more fervent as he becomes better acquainted with his Lord.[21]

It was also a Friday evening when I first heard about Jesus' Second Coming when I was living in Baghdad, Iraq. When I got home that evening, I went to my room on the second story of our house. I opened the curtains and gazed into the sky, waiting for Jesus to come. But I remember the feeling of disappointment when He didn't.

This memory sparked a familiar yearning for Jesus' return. It was not that I did not believe in the Second Coming, but I had lost my anticipation for it. As I wrestled through my feelings, I felt myself praying, "Lord, I travel 35 times every year, ministering to churches, pastors, and members." However, my thoughts trailed

---

[21] Ellen G. White, "Losing our First Love," *Advent Review and Sabbath Herald* 64/23 (June 7, 1887): 353, https://m.egwwritings.org/en/book/821.8222#8227 (accessed October 11, 2021).

off with the stark realization that I was trying to please and serve God without having a relationship with him. At this conclusion, I started to cry, and I found myself saying, "Lord, I do love You. Please restore my passion and the enthusiasm that I once had for You."

On that flight, I learned an eternal lesson. There is a big difference between "first love" and "stale love." In "first love," there is intensity, passion, excitement, and yearning. But in "stale love," one goes through the motions of doing some of these things, but not with fervency.

I felt the gentle prompting of the Holy Spirit reminding me, "I am more interested in your heart and your love for Me than in your accomplishments and the trips you make to minister to other people." He reminded me of the text in Matthew 3:17, "And a voice from heaven said, 'This is my Son, whom I love; with him I am well pleased.'" Jesus heard the voice before He had done anything. He had yet to heal any sick, restore sight, preach a sermon, or write a book. He heard the voice before any of this, because Jesus had the relationship with God. He belonged to Him and was connected to Him. I felt God was telling me, "I love you, whether you do 35 trips or not. I want that relationship you had with Me at the beginning. I want you to restore your first love to Me."

Like the Church of Ephesus, the Lord asked me to do three specific things to strengthen my relationship with Him.

REMEMBER, REPENT, REPEAT

Outwardly, the church of Ephesus appeared to be a very spiritual church. It was very active in the work of God. The members toiled for the Lord, endured hardship, were doctrinally sound, and took a strong stand against the deeds of the Nicolaitans (Rev 2:2-3, 6). Nevertheless, there was something wrong. They were guilty of a sin that is hard to detect: losing your first love. But the Lord, who knows our hearts, counseled them to do three things that were desperately needed to reestablish their closeness and walk with Him. They needed to remember, repent, and repeat the things they did at the beginning of their relationship with God.

This is a very important lesson for God's people at any time in history, but especially for our performance-oriented society. It is a warning that if we are not careful, we can lose our spiritual health and vitality, existing in a condition in which we live, love, and serve Him, and slip into mere orthodoxy.

The three things the church of Ephesus needed are the things we need today:

REMEMBER

Jesus gave the Church of Ephesus three counsels to restore their love and deep relationship with Him. The first one is to remember the way things used to be. "Remember therefore from where you have fallen; repent and do the first works, or else I will come to you quickly and remove your lampstand from its place —unless you repent" (Rev 2:5, NKJV). This is a call to reflect, to go back and recall the past. The Savior is saying, "Remember the way it used to be in your relationship with Me."[22]

When the Prodigal Son was in an utterly desperate situation, the first step in his restoration to sonship was remembering the goodness of his father and what life was like back in his father's home (Luke 15:17-19). This is always the first step in getting back to where we should be with the Lord.

When I started to know and fall in love with Jesus early on in my life, I was determined to get my own Bible. I wanted to read it for myself and have Jesus change me like He changed Peter, Paul, John, and others. But getting my first Bible turned out to be a challenging endeavor.

At that time in Bagdad, where I lived, it was very difficult and complicated to get a Bible. It would cost about $100, and sometimes it took up to a year to get one. I was about 16 when I wanted to own my own Bible. I didn't want to ask the church to give me one, because I didn't want to cost them money. I wanted to work for my own Bible so that it would be special to me. I worked hard for my dad and earned $100 and gave it to the government, registering my name to get a Bible. After 8 months, I got a notice that my Bible

---

[22] The Greek word is *mnēmoneuō*, which is translated "remember." https://www.blueletterbible.org/kjv/Rev/2/5-7/t_conc_1169005 (accessed January 29, 2021).

was ready to pick up. After school one day, I went to pick it up. I was so excited that I immediately went home, hoping to read it.

My mother, who was a very loving woman, was also very strict when it came to homework. We couldn't do anything—no television, no sports, no playing outside—unless our homework was done first. She would always help us and make sure we did it correctly. I got home around 4 P.M. after picking up my Bible and worked on my homework until 10 P.M. My mom inspected my work and then told my brother and me it was time for bed. I wanted to read my Bible, so after my brother had fallen asleep, I went to the kitchen and got a flashlight. I got back in bed with my Bible, pulled the covers over my head, and turned on the flashlight. Someone had told me to start reading in the book of John. I fumbled my way through and found it. I just happened to land on John 8:12, which reads, "When Jesus spoke again to the people, He said, 'I am the light of the world. Whoever follows me will never walk in darkness, but will have the light of life.'" When I read these words, I was filled with so much joy and excitement that my heart started beating really quickly. My eyes were filled with sparkle, and I determined in my heart that Jesus would be the light of my life!

As I was immersed in reading, I didn't notice that my mom had gone to the kitchen to prepare the meals for the next day. On her way back to her bedroom, she decided to check on us. When she opened our door, she saw the beam of light shining through the blanket. She was terrified, wondering what her son was reading. She pulled back the blanket and to her surprise, she found me reading my Bible. She let out a huge sigh of relief and said, "You have 20 minutes to read, then go to sleep."

That was my first encounter with reading the Bible, and I fell in love with the Word of God. After this, I read it consistently and with passion. I looked forward to reading it every day! I learned all of the stories of the life and teachings of Jesus, the stories of Acts, the teachings of the Apostle Paul, and all the stories of the Old Testament. The result was that I fell in love more deeply and passionately with my Lord and Savior Jesus Christ. I want to live that experience again. On that journey on the plane, I prayed that God would restore the experience that I remembered so dearly.

REPENT

The Greek word used in the text is *metanoeō*, which is translated "repent."[23] This word means to change the mind or one's decision. "It means to recognize one's previous decision, opinion, or condition as wrong, and to accept and move toward a new and right path in its place."[24] Repentance includes confessing your sins, changing your direction, and going a different way.

On my defining, paradigm-shifting plane ride back, I reached a new understanding of how the Lord loves me and accepts me not because of my performance, but because I belong to Him. I remember praying, "Lord, I repent of whatever I have done, and I ask You to restore my first love for You." I felt good at the end of that trip and found renewed excitement and enthusiasm for God. I was so excited about what had happened to me that I wanted to share it with others. The following day, I shared what had happened with all of the classes I taught. At the end of the classes, I had many students tell me that they could identify with the experience and were moved to ask God to rekindle their love for Him. Maybe you as the reader have had similar experiences of losing your first love. If so, now is the time to ask God to restore the passion you once had for Him. A first step could be simply repenting of your current state of spiritual disengagement and moving toward the path of spiritual health and vitality.

I had been spiritually very busy, but my encounter with God and subsequent repentance made me move toward becoming spiritually healthy. In the Christian life, we may stay very busy with Christian activities such as reading the Bible, attending church, giving money, or serving others, but without a passionate love for God, we end up living a life "having a form of godliness but denying its power" (2 Tim 3:5). My prayer is that you will have a similar experience where God can restore your passion, excitement, and first love for Him.

---

[23] https://www.blueletterbible.org/kjv/Rev/2/5-7/t_conc_1169005 (accessed January 29, 2021).

[24] https://bible.org/seriespage/3-message-ephesus-rev-21-7 (accessed January 29, 2021).

REPEAT

"Do the deeds you did at first." This is not a call to more Christian service or to renewed Christian activity. The church of Ephesus had plenty of that. Then what does the Lord mean when He asks, "Consider how far you have fallen! Repent and do the things you did at first"? And how does the message apply to us today?

The appeal of Jesus to the Church of Ephesus is to do the first things they did when they fell in love with Him. These include honest confession of sin, and repentance, prayer, Bible study, reading, meditation, memorization, fellowship with believers, being occupied with Christ, and refocusing all of our life on Him (see Mark 3:14; 6:30-32; John 15:4-8; Ps 119).

There are three things I hate. I hate bowling. I dislike Indian cuisine (I love Indian people and India, but I do not like spicy food), and I abhor camping. My idea of camping is to stay in the Hilton.

When I was first dating my wife Denise, I went to her dorm one day at Walla Walla College and asked her what she wanted to do. She said, "Let's go bowling." I said, "Sure, I would love to!" (Though I hated bowling, I loved being with her.)

A few weeks later, I asked her, "Do you want to go out to eat?" She said, "Yes, let's go to this Indian restaurant." I said, "With you, I like going to any restaurant in the world."

A few weeks later, she came to me and said, "My family is going camping this weekend. Would you like to go with us?" I said, "I am hoping one day camping will be one of my favorite activities in the world. Let's go."

When you love someone, you want to be with them because love will change you. Over the years, I even came to like bowling and tolerate camping. (Indian food still does not sit well with me.) I must repeat these loving acts with my wife to strengthen our relationship. By the same token, we need to do the same with Christ. When you delight in God, He will give you the desires of your heart, and your heart will want to do the things that are pleasing in His sight, because His love will change you (see Ps 37:4).

CONCLUSION

If forsaking your "first love" can happen to the church at Ephesus, it can happen to you or me. I have seen preachers, elders, deacons, Sabbath School teachers, and members forsake their first love. How do we protect ourselves from this danger?

The answer is found in a simple statement from Jesus in the Sermon on the Mount: "'But seek first the kingdom of God and His righteousness, and all these things shall be added to you'" (Matt 6:33, NKJV). We must always put God, His kingdom, and His righteousness above everything else. As we remember Jesus' love, we will seek Him, repent of those things that have replaced our love for Him, and repeat those things which we first did in our relationship with Him. After all, Jesus also bids us to "Love the Lord your God with all your heart and with all your soul and with all your strength and with all your mind"; and, "Love your neighbor as yourself" (Luke 10:27).[25] Ellen G. White says that God does not want anything less than our wholehearted devotion and love for him.

> God will accept nothing less than the whole heart. Happy are they who from the commencement of their religious life have been true to their first love, growing in grace and the knowledge of our Lord Jesus Christ. The sure result of their intercourse and fellowship with their beloved Lord, will be to increase their piety, their purity, their fervor. They are receiving a divine education, and this is illustrated in a life of fervor, of diligence and zeal.[26]

God's love for us is so deep and powerful that He promises never to leave us or forsake us. He promises always to be near, no matter what our circumstances are. The experience of this kind of love will keep us in a deep and abiding love with Him.

A couple that has been married for a long time does not always have the same thrill of excitement they had when they first started

---

[25] See Deuteronomy 6:5 and Leviticus 19:18.

[26] Ellen G. White, "Losing our First Love," *Advent Review and Sabbath Herald* 64/23 (June 7, 1887): 353, https://m.egwwritings.org/en/book/821.8222#8227 (accessed October 11, 2021).

dating. That is to be expected and is okay as long as that excitement has matured into a depth of love that makes it even better. We should not always expect to have the exact same excitement we had when everything was brand new in our Christian walk. But the newness should transition into a depth that makes the first love even stronger.

The counsel of Jesus to the Church of Ephesus and to us today is to remember, repent, and repeat. Make the decision today to reclaim your first love. Ask the Lord to rekindle the passion and excitement you once felt for Him. Take inventory of the ways that routine spiritual busyness has slipped into your life, and replace it with spiritual health such as experiencing God's presence every day and living in the transformative power of God's love. This might look like going to bed a little earlier so you can meet God in the morning, or praying a bold prayer, expecting God to show up, if you've felt that God is distant. Meanwhile, ask God to open your eyes to the ways you need to repent of the things that are hindering your spiritual walk. If you do this, you will be partnering with God and what He wants to do in your life. "He has shown you, O mortal, what is good. And what does the Lord require of you? To act justly and to love mercy and to walk humbly with your God" (Mic 6:8).

CHAPTER 18

CAUGHT IN A CONFLICT: THE MOTIF OF VICTORY IN REVELATION

Laszlo Gallusz

We live in a world characterized by struggle for influence and power over the world. Nation rises against nation and kingdom rises against kingdom, as Jesus said they would (Matt 24:7). Who will rule the world and who will have which role in the system are key questions for many political moves in the west as well as in the east. For those wrestling in the arenas of power, victory is variously defined. Different methods and instruments are used in order to "win" on the public scene: politicians "win" in public elections, nations "win" in wars, autocrats seek to "win" people to buy into their truth system, or they simply destroy those who refuse to be aligned with their agenda.[1] Victory is evidently a concept that has far-reaching political, sociological, economic, but not less significant spiritual implications.

THEOLOGICAL CONTEXT: THE POWER STRUGGLE IN REVELATION

The book of Revelation is a book about power, namely about a cosmic confrontation over the legitimate useof power.[2] The key

---

[1] Stephen L. Homcy, "'To Him Who Overcomes': A Fresh Look at What 'Victory' Means for the Believer According to the Book of Revelation", *Journal of the Evangelical Theological Society*, 38/2 (1995), 193.

[2] For the cosmic conflict motif in Revelation, see Sigve K. Tonstad, *Saving God's Reputation: The Theological Function of Pistis Iesou in the Cosmic Narratives of Revelation* (London: T&T Clark International, 2006); Steven Grabiner, *Revelation's Hymns: Commentary on the Cosmic Conflict* (London: Bloomsbury T&T Clark, 2015).

question around which the drama pictured in the book revolves is: Who is the legitimate ruler of the universe? Opposed to the throne of God (ch. 4), the *axis mundi* of the created order, is the throne of Satan (2:13). The conflict between the two power centers is central for the theological outlook of the book in which reality is pictured in sharply dualistic terms, stressing that there is no middle ground. The human choice between good and evil is focused on the matter of allegiance—allegiance to the kingdom of God, or allegiance to the kingdom of the world. There is no dual citizenship in New Jerusalem and Babylon.[3]

The theme of holy war, which is the basic background of the conquering motif, is rooted in this dualistic emphasis: in the contrast between "the kingdom of our Lord" and "the kingdom of the world" (11:15, NRSV). These two realms are not only alternatives, but oppositional realms that are in conflict. They both have their own armies (14:4-5 vs. 19:19). The cosmic war is over the "throne," which not only in Revelation but also in the Old Testament and Ancient Near East literature is the symbol of power and authority.[4] So, the book's basic theological framework is the notion of a great controversy, and the question that naturally arises between the lines is: Who will conquer in the cosmic power struggle, having a legitimate authority?

The motif of victory is of major significance for the structure and theology of Revelation. More than a century ago Swete noted that "the book is a record and a prophecy of victories won by Christ and the Church."[5] It is a work written as a prophetic exhortation for the Lamb's followers to triumph in Him. The significance of the motif for Revelation clearly surfaces in some basic details about the use of the terminology itself. First, the term *nikaō* ("be victor," "to overcome," "to conquer"), which drives the motif throughout the book, occurs in different grammatical forms designating "victory" or "superiority," whether in the

[3] On dualism as rhetorical technique in apocalyptic literature, see e.g. Gregory Stevenson, *A Slaughtered Lamb: Revelation and the Apocalyptic Response to Evil and Suffering* (Abilene, TX: Abilene Christian University Press, 2013), 98-102.

[4] On the theological significance of the throne motif in Revelation, see Laszlo Gallusz, *The Throne Motif in the Book of Revelation* (London: Bloomsbury T&T Clark, 2014).

[5] Henry Barclay Swete, *The Apocalypse of St John: The Greek Text with Introduction Notes and Indices*, 3d ed. (London: Macmillan, 1911), 29.

physical, legal, or metaphorical sense, and whether in mortal conflict or peaceful competition.[6] Second, the term occurs 28 times in the New Testament, 17 of them in Revelation. So, 60.7% of the New Testament *nikaō* references are in the last book of the biblical canon. Third, these references appear in ten chapters (nearly half of the chapters of Revelation), distributed throughout the whole book, from its first vision to its last. They often appear at strategically significant locations.

The interpretation of the motif of victory necessitates establishing the "big picture" of its use in Revelation. This requires tracing the progression of the motif throughout the book by giving attention to each individual reference. Therefore, the analysis of the *nikaō* references should start from the beginning of the book, and it should give attention to the gradual development of the motif that builds towards the climax at the end of the book.

CALLED TO OVERCOME: THE PROMISES TO THE CONQUERORS (REV 2-3)

The first seven references to the motif of victory are found in the first vision of Revelation. This vision consists of seven messages of the resurrected Christ to historical churches in Asia Minor at the end of the first century c.e. (chs. 2-3). Aune argues that the genre of the messages is "that of the royal or imperial edict."[7] If this is the background, Christ addressed the churches as a king speaking to His subjects. This feature points to His true sovereignty, which is in contrast to the quasi-sovereigns acting in the book by contesting God's unique place in the universe.

There are number of reasons to believe that the seven churches of Revelation 2-3 are pointing beyond the historical situation of the first century and are intended to represent the universal church throughout the Christian age. First, the number seven is woven into the very fabric of the book, symbolizing completeness.

---

[6] For an in-depth word-study of *nikaō*, see e.g. Moisés Silva (revision ed.), *"nikaō,"* in *New International Dictionary of New Testament Theology and Exegesis*, 3 (Grand Rapids, MI: Zondervan, 2014), 391-396.

[7] D. E. Aune, "The Form and Function of the Proclamations to the Seven Churches (Revelation 2-3)," *New Testament Studies*, 36/2 (1990), 183.

There were many other Christian churches in first-century Asia Minor, but choosing only seven of them as addressees conveys an emphasis on a universal scope. Second, the same refrain at the end of each message ("Let anyone who has an ear listen to what the Spirit is saying to the churches," NRSV) indicates that all churches were to heed each message, although each was also specifically addressed. Third, church history teaches us that the issues the seven churches faced in Asia Minor at the end of the first century are to a greater or lesser extent the same problems that Christian congregations have faced in all generations in the last two thousand years: the presence of heresy, internal divisions, lack of eagerness, and in some places, persecution. These problems are with us still today in various forms.

In each of the seven messages the resurrected Jesus provides an analysis of the situation of the addressed church. Seven times He says "I know," indicating His perfect knowledge about the situation of His people. He says, "I know your deeds" (2:2, 9, 13, 19; 3:1, 8, 15). He assures the church in Pergamon that He knows where the church lives (2:13), while the church in Smyrna is made certain that Jesus is aware of the tribulations it is facing (2:9). Whatever the content of the analysis, the message concludes with a promise or promises related to "the inheritance of salvation blessings."[8]

However, these promises are not of a universal nature. Conquering is specified as the condition for inheriting salvation. This is repeated in all of the messages (2:7, 11, 17, 26; 3:5, 12, 21). Significantly, in each reference the term "to conquer" occurs in present participle form (*ho nikōn*). Since the present participle is a mood in Greek that signifies an ongoing experience, the feature indicates the dynamic character of the Christian discipleship: overcoming is expected to be a constant experience, a lifestyle of the church.

It has been observed that there is a progression in the number of promises to the churches. Each church receives one more promise than the preceding one, starting with Ephesus, which is given only one promise (2:7). So, there is a clear and constant

---

[8] G. K. Beale, *The Book of Revelation: A Commentary on the Greek Text* (Grand Rapids, MI: Eerdmans, 1999), 234.

intensification through the messages. However, the last church (Laodicea) is given only one promise instead of the expected seven—and this breaks the pattern.[9] The change of the dynamics is intentional. It generates a sense of climax, stressing the emphatic character of the promise that concludes the line of promises: "To him who overcomes I will grant to sit with Me on My throne, as I also overcame and sat down with My Father on His throne" (3:21).[10] Sitting with God on His throne indicates not only a ruling position in the messianic kingdom, but receiving everything God could grant His children, including first of all His closeness and trust.

According to a legend, when Alexander the Great was at the high point of his rule, a young man wished to see the mighty king one day. By a miracle, he was able to enter the king's palace, since no one noticed him. He even managed to find the throne room, but when he opened its doors, no one was in it. In the middle of the throne room, he saw the throne of Alexander and his crown on it. Then he got a crazy idea. He entered and sat on the throne of the most powerful man of his time, putting the kingly crown on his head. At that moment Alexander the Great entered into the throne room. Being shocked by the sight, he immediately ordered the execution of the young man. For earthly rulers— whether ancient or contemporary—the touching of their "throne" is a highly sensitive issue. They are often ready for war or great compromises rather than giving up their thrones.

God is radically different. He expresses His joy over the salvation of His people by His readiness to share even His throne instead of protecting it. The scene is telling of the value He sees in human beings created in His own image, who are more precious to Him than anything in this world. While the promise of Revelation 3:21 communicates God's strong desire to see us in His kingdom, it also sets forth conquering as a condition for inheriting His promises.

A number of questions arise at this point in the story line of Revelation: Who is the example to be followed in conquering? Who provides God's people with relevant resources for conquering?

---

[9] Jon Paulien, *The Deep Things of God* (Hagerstown, MD: Review and Herald, 2004), 116.

[10] Unless otherwise noted, Bible quotations are from the New King James Version.

Which guidelines are to be followed so that the conquering by God's people might be legitimate? The answers to these questions are given in the next vision.

FOUNDATION FOR VICTORY: THE TRIUMPH OF THE SLAUGHTERED LAMB (REV 5:5-6)

In Revelation 5, into the scene steps the central character of the book of Revelation: the Lamb. His characterization is the rhetorical center-point of the chapter:

> Then one of the elders said to me, 'Do not weep. See, the Lion of the tribe of Judah, the Root of David, has conquered [*enikēsen*], so that he can open the scroll and its seven seals.' Then I saw between the throne and the four living creatures and among the elders a Lamb standing as if it had been slaughtered, having seven horns and seven eyes, which are the seven spirits of God sent out into all the earth (Rev 5:5-6, NRSV).

The basic event pictured in Revelation 5 is the enthronement of Jesus Christ.[11] This event took place after His ascension; the pouring out of the Holy Spirit at Pentecost was the visible sign of it. The basic characteristic of the Lion-Lamb messianic figure is that He "conquered" (*enikēsen*, 5:5).The Greek expression in the aorist is emphatic: the Lion's worthiness is rooted in the fact of His conquering. This triumph is the rhetorical center-point of the chapter. While no direct object of conquering is supplied in the sentence, the fact of conquering implies a battle of some sort, a struggle with God's enemies.[12]

The apostle John, hearing about a conquering Lion, turned to see this mighty triumphant kingly figure who is able to solve the epic, cosmic problem posed at the beginning of the chapter (5:1-3). He saw, however, a Lamb standing "as though it had been slain" (5:6). The scene has a shocking effect. The text indicates that the

---

[11] For a detailed argument, see Ranko Stefanovic, *The Background and Meaning of the Sealed Book of Revelation 5* (Berrien Springs, MI: Andrews University Press, 1996).

[12] Robert G. Bratcher and Howard A. Hatton, *A Handbook on The Revelation to John* (New York: United Bible Societies, 1993), 100.

Lamb had marks on its body which showed that it had been killed, but in reality, it was alive. This is a reference to the sacrificial death of Jesus. The Lion of Judah is a well-known Old Testament messianic title (Gen 49:9) that points to Christ's overcoming of the enemy. The imagery of the Passover Lamb,[13] however, redefines the nature of Christ's victory. Juxtaposing of imageries is a discernible pattern elsewhere in the book: the imagery placed directly after an "audition" is given in order to interpret its nature. While the Lion imagery stresses the fact of Christ's victory (He "has conquered" [NRSV]), the Lamb imagery defines the manner of His victory ("as though it had been slain"). The perfect passive participle "had been slain" (*esphagmenon*) points to the effect, the present result of the Lamb's sacrifice. As Mounce notes, "In one brilliant stroke John portrays the central theme of the New Testament revelation—victory through sacrifice."[14]

The Lamb of Revelation 5 is not a helpless Lamb who suffered death as a victim. The fact that He has seven horns (a symbol of perfect power) and seven eyes (perfect knowledge) indicates His omnipotence and omniscience. Yet, He submits voluntarily for the sake of the salvation of humankind, and His seeming defeat on the cross is actually, from the divine perspective, a victory. The victory of the Lamb is not based on violence or manipulation; it is a victory of values. The cross demonstrates that love is a greater power than hatred, and evil is to be defeated by good.[15] Thus, God's people find their example in the methods of the Lamb rather than the methods of the powers of this world, which act as beasts who aggressively seek to control others, persecuting people who think differently and killing those who are a threat to their kingdom. The way of the Lamb is fundamentally different: it is focused on values that are rooted in the cross.

No wonder the heavenly scene of Revelation 5 is one of the most joyous scenes in the New Testament. The Lamb is praised by the twenty-four elders, by the four creatures, and by "myriads

---

[13] Revelation's imagery of the Lamb also recalls the notion of Isaiah 53:7: "He was led as a lamb to the slaughter" (NKJV).

[14] Robert H. Mounce, *The Book of Revelation*, New International Commentary on the New Testament, 17 (Grand Rapids, MI: Eerdmans, 1977), 144.

[15] See Romans 12:21.

of myriads and thousands of thousands" of angels, on equal terms with God the Father for the salvation He has achieved through His sacrifice (5:8-14, NRSV). This scene, however, is not the end of the story. It is only the launching scene for what will follow: the Lamb has conquered, and He has a conquering program for His church.

SURPRISES ON THE PATH OF CHRISTIAN DISCIPLESHIP: BEING CONQUERED (REV 11:7; 13:7)

After the heavenly scene of Revelation 5 that presents the victory of the Lamb, the stage is set for the victory of God's people. After such a brilliant introduction, one would expect the continuation and progressing of the victory without major difficulties. As human beings, however, we know from experience that not everything in life is triumphant. It is unrealistic to expect always to jump from one peak to another. The reality is that life holds many challenges and surprises for us. Sometimes it is our fate to go through dark valleys.

In tracing the motif of victory in Revelation, we encounter a shocking moment: God's people are defeated by evil powers. In Revelation 13 the regime of the beast puts God's people in a precarious situation: "Also it was allowed to make war on the saints and to conquer them. It was given authority over every tribe and people and language and nation" (13:7, NRSV).[16] Since in the apocalyptic literature four is the number of the Earth, indicating universality, the fourfold formula ("every tribe and people and language and nation") points to the universal character of the world order established by the beast (cf. Rev 14:6).

It is significant, however, that the beast possesses authority because it is "allowed" to him. The aorist passive (*edothē*, "was given") assumes an authority above the authority of the beast, which "allows" him to act. This grammatical feature is known as a "divine passive" (*passivum divinum*), which assumes that God is the ultimate acting subject who sets boundaries for the actions of the beast. Divine passive is, therefore, more than a grammatical feature: it is a theological category that stresses the idea

---

[16] Similarly, a beast coming from the bottomless pit overcomes the two witnesses after they finish their testimony (11:7).

that God is to be viewed as the ultimate power and control overthe reality. Due to the strong emphasis on God's sovereignty in Revelation, divine passive is a feature repeatedly present throughout the entire book.[17]

The basic implication of the use of the divine passive in relation to the victory of the beast over God's people is that this conquering only seems to be a victory. In light of the cosmic context, whatever happens to God's people on the earth serves a higher purpose in the realization of God's plan. Often we don't know how it will serve this purpose, and the experience is often painful to go through, but we are assured that God has the ultimate authority and that He is in control of things—though there are dimensions of evil unknown to us.

This surprising aspect of Revelation's motif of victory indicates that the path of discipleship is unpredictable. It is often full of surprises. There are periods in our lives in which we go through experiences that bring us pain and disillusionment. These experiences serve as reminders of our limitations as finite human beings and show us how dependent on His grace we are. This is one of the main reasons why twice in the heart of the Cosmic Conflict vision the need for endurance is emphasized —endurance that is seen as a principal virtue of God's people, on the same level with keeping God's commandments and holding fast to the faith of Jesus (Rev 13:10; 14:12).

THE PATTERN FOR VICTORY: THE TWO PILLARS (REV 12:11)

While we can trace a clear progression in the development of the motif of victory in Revelation, until chapter 12 it is not clearly defined whom or what God's people are to conquer. Bauckham argues convincingly that the verb "to conquer" is intentionally left without an object until chapter 12, "because it is only in chapters 12-13 that the principal enemies of God, who must be defeated to make way for his kingdom, are introduced."[18] Also, leaving the object of conquest intentionally open indicates

---

[17] Revelation 6:2, 4 [2×], 8, 11; 7:2; 8:2-3; 9:1, 3, 5; 11:1-2; 12:14; 16:8; 19:8; 20:4.

[18] Richard Bauckham, *The Theology of the Book of Revelation* (Cambridge: Cambridge University Press, 1993), 88-89.

that God's people are to conquer everything that is opposed to God, His values, and His kingdom.

Revelation 12 provides the key for understanding the cosmic conflict. This chapter identifies the archenemy of God and His people, the antagonist to God's purposes, who is the source of the conflict and is "the sum total of evil."[19] His character and his intentions are openly disclosed: "that serpent of old, called the Devil and Satan, who deceives the whole world" (12:9). He is not only a frustrated foe, but also a mortally wounded enemy who "'knows that he has a short time'" (12:12). More significant than the characterization of the enemy, however, is that a clear answer is given to the question, How are God's people to conquer him?

Revelation 12:11 provides a pattern for victory for God's people. The text says: "'And they overcame him by the blood of the Lamb and by the word of their testimony, and they did not love their lives to the death'" (12:11). This text should be underlined in red in the Bibles of all students of Revelation, since it is one of the most important texts in the book. It makes clear that the victory of God's people is achieved through two means: (1) "by the blood of the Lamb" and (2) "by the word of their testimony."

ON THE SEA OF GLASS: THE CELEBRATION OF THE CONQUERORS (REV 15:2)

If God's people follow the pattern given in Revelation 12:11, the following words are going to be fulfilled in their lives:

> And I saw something like a sea of glass mingled with fire, and those who have the victory over the beast, over his image and over his mark and over the number of his name, standing on the sea of glass, having harps of God. They sing the song of Moses, the servant of God, and the song of the Lamb, saying: 'Great and marvelous are Your works, Lord God Almighty! Just and true are Your ways, O King of the saints!' (Rev 15:2-3).

---

[19] Peter A. Abir, *The Cosmic Conflict of the Church: An Exegetico-Theological Study of Revelation 12, 7-12* (Frankfurt am Main: Peter Lang, 1996), 105.

The vision pictures a heavenly scene in which the redeemed praise God. The basic feature in their characterization is that they are conquerors: they "have the victory over the beast, over his image and over his mark and over the number of his name." The fourfold formula indicates the complexity of the conflict (there are many things to be conquered!), but it also has a universal ring (four objects of conquering). While the beast had been victorious over the redeemed, that victory only seemed to be a victory—it looked like a triumph only from an earthly perspective. From God's perspective, the lives of the redeemed have impacted the world, and *they* have been victorious. Finally, in Revelation 19-20, Jesus Himself brings final justice on the world and the devil. The enemies of God are ultimately defeated, and the saints reign with Jesus Christ.

THE CLIMAX: LIFE IN THE NEW CREATION (REV 21:7)

The motif of victory reaches its climax in the final vision of the book, which is the grand finale of the story line of the entire Bible: the vision of the New Jerusalem (Rev 21:1–22:5).[20] The promises given to the conquerors in chapters 2-3 find their ultimate fulfillment in chapters 21-22. "Although the promises are phrased differently in each letter, they are all versions of the final promise of the book to the 'conquerors'" stated in 21:7.[21] The text that sums up all the promises reads: "He who overcomes shall inherit all things, and I will be his God and he shall be My son" (21:7).

The text defines precisely the identity of God's people. Each person belonging to God's people is qualified as an overcomer. To each, the greatest reward is the incredible fact that "I will be his God and he shall be My son." This phrase is a well-known Old Testament covenant formula. It sums up the Abrahamic covenant (Gen 17:7), the Mosaic covenant (Exod 6:7) and the Davidic

---

[20] William J. Dumbrell (*The End of the Beginning: Revelation 21-22 and the Old Testament* [Homebush West, NSW: Lancer, 1985]) convincingly argues that Rev 21-22 is constructed to demonstrate the fulfillment of the major ideas of salvation history. He traces the historical development of the themes of New Jerusalem, new temple, new covenant, new Israel, and new creation, pointing out how they climax in the New Jerusalem vision. As Dumbrell demonstrates, the vision appears not only as an appropriate way to finish Revelation, but also as a grand conclusion of the entire Bible's story line.

[21] Beale, *Revelation*, 234.

covenant (2 Sam 7:14). It points to the fact that the greatest reward of God's people is not a material treasure of any kind (like a house in the New Jerusalem or life in a city with golden streets), but the reality of the covenant relationship with God. Already now we are adopted as God's children, having the foretaste of the final joy of the fellowship with God (Rom 8:14-17), but we are looking forward to a day when we can see God face to face and the consequences of sin will be undone (Rev 22:3-4).

In our discussions about the character of the eternal life, we often lose sight of the essence, focusing wrongly on some secondary details. Eternal life is not like an extended holiday on a tropical island, which lasts for millions of years. Neither is it a religious version of a chocolate hill given to children, which they can eat without limitations and consequences. According to Revelation 21:7, the essence of the eternal life is living in a covenant relationship with God—this is the true reward, which brings the greatest fulfillment to the redeemed. This covenant life also has practical dimensions. It involves some kind of serving, since giving is an essential component of love, and love is basic to God's character.

CONCLUSION

We are living between the cross and the second coming of Christ. In practical terms, this means that we are involved in a war of cosmic dimensions; we cannot run away from this fact. Paul says: "For we do not wrestle against flesh and blood, but against principalities, against powers, against the rulers of the darkness of this age, against spiritual hosts of wickedness in the heavenly places" (Eph 6:12). The book of Revelation is an extended commentary on this idea: the cosmic conflict.

We are assured that Christ has conquered, but that is not the end of the story. He has a conquering program for His church. The pattern for the church's conquering involves two essential aspects: (1) relying on the blood of Jesus; and (2) giving an authentic witness in a culture that is directed by different values.

In this life we live in a crossfire. In practical terms, seeking victory in Jesus means that we will love not our earthly lives, but the Author of life. It also means that we will not measure success by human, earthly standards or victory by earthly gains, but in terms of our alignment with God's plan to advance His kingdom. It further means that we will not sacrifice the testimony of Jesus on the altar of compromise and convenience.

Life is unpredictable. God, however, invites us to cooperate with him in bringing His plan to reality. At times it is challenging to be part of the "church militant," but Revelation provides encouragement to God's people that if they persevere on the path of discipleship and demonstrate undivided loyalty to the interests of their Lord, one day as a "church triumphant" they will see God face to face, praising Him in the new creation.

CHAPTER 19

REVELATION 14 - THE PULSE OF ADVENTIST IDENTITY, MESSAGE, AND MISSION: THE CONTEXT

Ganoune Diop

It is our privilege and honor to be ambassadors of Christ, agents of reconciliation between God and the whole human family. This is how the Apostle Paul in 2 Corinthians 5 envisioned his main function. One of our desires is to engage in conversations with the whole world regarding God's last testament, the book of Revelation, especially Revelation 14, the climax of the central section of the book.

At the outset it is crucial to bear in mind that Revelation 14 is part of a book—actually, it is located at the center of the book of Revelation, whose main purpose is the preparation of the church and of the world for the Second Coming. From the first prophecy in Revelation 1:7 to the last promise and the last prayer (Rev 22:20), the hope of the Second Coming is prevalent. The proclamation of the three angels' messages is immediately followed by the Second Coming of Jesus Christ (Rev 14:14).

Revelation 14 is a defining text among Seventh-day Adventists. It articulates the parameters within which to think about the Adventist identity, message, and mission. It encapsulates the scope of the mission entrusted to our care, the content of the message we share, and the pulse of the identity of the end time Seventh-day Adventist movement we claim.

The importance and universal nature of the three angels' messages make them an inseparable part of Adventist consciousness, missional endeavor, and ethical imperatives. Ellen White wrote:

Every feature of the third angel's message is to be proclaimed in all parts of the world. . . . This message is a
testing message. Received into honest hearts, it will
prove an antidote for all the world's sins and sorrows.
No conditions of climate, of poverty, or ignorance, or of
prejudice can hinder its efficiency, or lessen its adaptability
to the needs of mankind.[1]

She further wrote that:

The third angel's message reveals the great saving truth
for this time. Its truths are constantly unfolding, and it
is God's design that even the children and youth shall
understand intelligently what God requires, that they
may distinguish between righteousness and sin, between
obedience and disobedience.[2]

There is more to Revelation 14 than meets the eye.

CLEARING SOME MISUNDERSTANDINGS IN DELINEATING THE MEANING OF THE THREE ANGELS' MESSAGES

Seventh-day Adventists have identified important features
found in the fourteenth chapter of the book of Revelation. For
example:

THE MENTION OF THE COMMANDMENTS OF GOD

Besides the explicit general reference to the commandments
of God in Revelation 14:12, Seventh-day Adventists have noted
wording in this section that refers to the Sabbath in particular.
It is found in the mention of creation in the first angel's message,
using words drawn from the Sabbath commandment in Exodus
20. The insistence on God's sovereignty in reference to creation
led Seventh-day Adventists to connect this message with the
importance of the Sabbath as a sign of loyalty to God. Given the

---

[1] Ellen G White, Manuscript 75, 1906, "A Caution against Heavy Investment in Food
Manufacture," September 29, 1906, 3, published in Ellen G. White, *Manuscript Releases*, vol. 9
(Silver Spring, MD: Ellen G. White Estate, 1990), 292.

[2] Ellen G. White, Manuscript 67, 1909, "A High Standard," October 7, 1909, published in
Manuscript Releases, vol. 9, 292.

context of the three angels' messages just prior to the Second Coming, Seventh-day Adventists have not found it farfetched to envision the Sabbath as playing an eschatological role as a sign of allegiance. This aspect of Adventist belief is present in the name chosen to designate the movement: "Seventh-day Adventist."

THE FAITH OF JESUS

The other important feature, especially in the third angel's message, is the meaning of the "faith of Jesus."

Regarding these two key issues, when asked what the faith of Jesus in the third angel's message was, Ellen White gave a clear, unequivocal answer:

The commandments of God have been proclaimed, but the faith of Jesus has not been proclaimed by Seventh-day Adventists as of equal importance, the law and the gospel going hand in hand.

She then stated the following:

What constitutes the faith of Jesus, that belongs to the third angel's message? Jesus becoming our sin-bearer that He might become our sin-pardoning Saviour. He was treated as we deserve to be treated. He came to our world and took our sins that we might take His righteousness. Faith in the ability of Christ to save us amply and fully and entirely is the faith of Jesus.[3]

A wonderful gospel understanding of the gift of Christ's righteousness is beautifully expressed in the following statement:

He died for us, and now He offers to take our sins and give us His righteousness. If you give yourself to Him, and accept Him as your Saviour, then, sinful as your life may have been, for His sake you are accounted righteous.

---

[3] Ellen G. White, Manuscript 24, 1888, in Ellen G. White, *Manuscript Releases*, vol. 12 (Silver Spring, MD: Ellen G. White Estate, 1993), 193.

Christ's character stands in place of your character, and you are accepted before God just as if you had not sinned.

More than this, Christ changes the heart. He abides in your heart by faith. You are to maintain this connection with Christ by faith and the continual surrender of your will to Him, and so long as you do this, He will work in you to will and to do according to His good pleasure. So you may say, 'The life which I now live in the flesh I live by the faith of the Son of God, who loved me, and gave Himself for me.' Galatians 2:20. . . . Then with Christ working in you, you will manifest the same spirit and do the same works—works of righteousness, obedience.

So, we have nothing in ourselves of which to boast. We have no ground for self-exaltation. Our only ground for hope is in the righteousness of Christ imputed to us, and in that wrought by His Spirit working in and through us.[4]

Imputed righteousness encapsulates the depth of the love of God and the gratitude it should constantly stir in the heart of anyone who genuinely embraces Jesus as Lord and Savior. This gift born from the depth of God's love is what prompted the Apostle Paul to exclaim that "the love of Christ compels us, because we judge thus: that if One died for all, then all died; and He died for all, that those who live should live no longer for themselves, but for Him who died for them and rose again" (2 Cor 5:14-15, NKJV).

It is in the development of this thought of Christ's substitutionary atonement that the Apostle Paul specifies that we are ambassadors for Christ, entrusted with the ministry of reconciliation (2 Cor 5:18-20).

THE GREAT CONTROVERSY

The context of Revelation 14 is that of the great controversy, a spiritual battle between God and the agencies of evil. Chapter 12 tells the story of an antagonism between Christ and Satan. Verse 7 specifies that there was war in heaven. This war moved to earth, where Christ became incarnate. The text shows Satan

---

[4] Ellen G. White, *Steps to Christ* (Mountain View, CA: Pacific Press, 1956), 62-63.

determined to destroy Christ and thus to prevent salvation from becoming a reality. To eradicate all signs pointing to Christ, Satan pursues the followers of Christ through persecution and deception and even succeeds in defeating the saints (e.g., the martyrs of the fifth seal and of Rev 13:7).

In Revelation 13 the dragon, Satan, uses religious and political entities by making them his allies in order to coerce, persecute, alienate, and kill the saints. Counterfeit entities try to mimic and to usurp God's sovereignty and authority. They are the main protagonists of Revelation 13.

In fact, Revelation 14 is thus a response to all this, calling God's people to show a resilient faith in the sovereignty of God through unwavering trust in Christ and obedience to the Holy Spirit. The repeated invitations to hear what the Spirit says to the churches are a testimony to this invitation to surrender to the Holy Spirit in the name of Christ, to the glory of the Father. (The Spirit speaks in Rev 14:13.)

The evil one and a third of the angels cast out from heaven invaded the earth, now an occupied territory, in order to sabotage and dehumanize people created in the image of God. The Spirit does the opposite, in re-humanizing humans created in the image of God. As we approach the Second Coming of Christ, the agencies of evil mobilize their forces to destroy the saints. They use any means they can to sever the bond between Christ and those created in Christ's image. Christ is the image of the invisible God. On this point Ellen White wrote the following:

"The agencies of evil are combining their forces and consolidating. They are strengthening for the last great crisis. Great changes are soon to take place in our world, and the final movements will be rapid ones."[5]

The Apostle John wrote that there were many antichrists, and on this basis he wrote, "we know that it is the last hour" (1 John 2:18).[6] One can foresee that before the Second Coming there would

---

[5] Ellen G. White. *Testimonies for the Church*, vol. 9 (Mountain View, CA: Pacific Press, 1948), 11.

[6] Unless otherwise noted, scripture quotations in this chapter are from the New American Standard Bible, 1995 edition.

be a similar multiplication and intensification of the work of the agencies of evil to deceive and to persecute. Spiritualism as a work of the evil spirits will become a worldwide phenomenon.

The intensifying of the great controversy as the end approaches is illustrated in the pouring out of the sixth bowl, one of the seven last plagues.

The sixth angel poured out his bowl on the great river, the Euphrates, and its water dried up, so that the way would be prepared for the kings from the east. And I saw coming out of the mouth of the dragon and out of the mouth of the beast and out of the mouth of the false prophet, three unclean spirits like frogs; for they are spirits of demons, performing signs, which go out to the kings of the whole world, to gather them together for the war of the great day of God, the Almighty. ("Behold, I am coming like a thief. Blessed is the one who stays awake and keeps his clothes, so that he will not walk about naked and men will not see his shame.") And they gathered them to the place which in Hebrew is called Har-Magedon. (Rev 16:12-16)

The time when the three angels' messages are given corresponds also to the time when three spirits of demons are spreading their messages for a final war in the great day of God, the Day of the Lord that the prophets foretold, when God will defeat the enemies of Christ and of His followers.

This spiritual controversy is the reason for the prophetic pronouncement of the second angel's message regarding of the fall of Babylon and the warnings in the third angel's message regarding the worship of the beast and his image and about receiving the mark of his name (Rev 14:11). The antidote to such drifting into idolatry, this worship of the beast, is the keeping of God's commandments and the faith of Jesus (Rev 14:12). These are the distinctive characteristics of those who receive the seal of God, His seal of protection (see Rev 7), the name of the Lamb and of His Father written on their foreheads, the mark of God instead of the mark of the beast, the seal of allegiance to God instead of the mark of the beast.

Revelation 14 redirects our whole life and lifestyle to center on the awareness of God's constant sovereignty, to live to glorify God, and to commit to worshiping God alone.

JESUS, THE GREAT CENTER OF ATTRACTION

Regarding the heart of the message we share, in connection with the three angels' messages, the Sabbath truth, and other truths in the message, Ellen White specifies the following:

> Of all professing Christians, Seventh-day Adventists should be foremost in uplifting Christ before the world. The proclamation of the third angel's message calls for the presentation of the Sabbath truth. This truth, with others included in this message, is to be proclaimed; but the great center of attraction, Christ Jesus, must not be left out. It is at the cross of Christ that mercy and truth meet together, and righteousness and peace kiss each other. The sinner must be led to look to Calvary; with the simple faith of a little child, he must trust in the merits of the Saviour, accepting His righteousness, believing in His mercy.[7]

Clearly, for Ellen G. White, the Sabbath truth and other aspects included in the third angel's message ought to be proclaimed; however, she insisted that the faith of Jesus, and Jesus' being the great center of attration, is the content of the third angel's message.

This means that the core of the Seventh-day Adventist mandate or mission is to uplift Jesus Christ before the world.

A NEED FOR A CLOSER LOOK AT THE TEXT

A text is a unique world with its own internal logic that functions as a thread that binds all its elements together. All the words of a given text participate in the making of meaning. Therefore, we need to identify as carefully and as comprehensively as possible all the elements of the text and make an inventory of how words are related to one another in a network, making a tapestry wonderfully woven into a comprehensible message. Reading a text can be conceived as at best discerning the networks within the text that show its internal coherence, and ultimately the unique perspectives, worldviews, and values it attempts to convey or use to convince the reader.

---

[7] Ellen G. White, *Gospel Workers* (Washington, DC: Review and Herald, 1915), 156-157.

Our study of Revelation 14 would gain from such attention to all its content. First then, from a methodological perspective, the reading strategy will be based on a decision to look at the text, nothing but the text, and the whole text. It is about describing its various components before interpreting its overall content. In other words, a diligent description is needed before venturing into the phase of interpretation.

Since Revelation 14 is not the only text in the book of Revelation, it will be helpful to identify and understand how it is related to the other texts, chapters, or sections, of the book.

Internally, the section in which the three angels' messages are located is one of the most rich and profound texts in the Bible.

Even a cursory look at the words used in chapters 14 and 15 reveals major themes of salvation history that are condensed into this section: creation, redemption, judgment, defeat of Satan, fall of God's enemies, demise of the persecutors and oppressors of God's people, the protection and sealing of God's people, the commandments of God, the faith of Jesus, a blessing and words of comfort from the Holy Spirit, the Coming of the "Son of Man" to harvest the earth, the wrath of God, an eschatological exodus, an antitypical day of judgment or of atonement, a warning and appeal not to share the fate of God's enemies, and allusions to the Exodus, to the death and resurrection of Jesus, and to the final festival, the Feast of Tabernacles, the festival of joy.

The issue of joy in this chapter is not new. Earlier, in Revelation 7, we had a clear reference to the Feast of Tabernacles in the explicit mention of the palm branches in the hands of the victors. The text specifies that no one can count the number of the victors. We note this amazing feature of salvation history. It is an assurance! God's mission will be successful. The redeemed from all nations, tribes, peoples, and tongues will be at that final post-tribulation, post-time-of-trouble, post-judgment occasion, joining the festival of victory standing before the throne of God and of the Lamb (Rev 7:9). God will succeed in His mission, and those who join God in His mission will also succeed, with God as the architect and fulfiller of the mission through His Holy Spirit.

MAPPING REVELATION 14: THE LARGER THEMATIC CONTEXT

When it comes to the gospel in the book of Revelation, there are significant parallels and thematic connections between the introduction of the book, chapters 4 and 5, chapters 10 and 11, and chapter 14.

THEMATIC CONNECTIONS

Chapter 10 begins with the mention of another mighty angel who cries out with a loud voice (10:1-3). The last mention before this of a powerful angel who proclaims with a loud voice is found in chapter 5:2. Moreover, the three angels' messages to the inhabitants of the earth also begin with the mention of another angel having an everlasting gospel to proclaim (14:6). There is therefore a close relationship between chapters 1, 5, 10, and 14. Moreover, from a thematic point of view, these chapters share the mention of the Creator God of the sky and all that it contains, the earth and all that it contains, and the sea and all that it contains (Rev 10:6; see Rev 4:11 and 14:7).

Connections with the Introduction of the book. When Jesus Christ, the subject and object of the book of Revelation, is first introduced, it is about the gospel. He is "the faithful witness, the firstborn of the dead, and the ruler of the kings of the earth" (Rev 1:5). He

> loves us and released us from our sins by His blood— and He has made us to be a kingdom, priests to His God and Father—to Him be the glory and the dominion forever and ever. Amen. BEHOLD HE IS COMING WITH THE CLOUDS, and every eye will see him, even those who pierced Him, and all the tribes of the earth will mourn over Him. So it is to be. Amen (Rev 1:5-7).

The gospel of good news is about the love of God, the salvation of God made available through faith in Christ's sacrifice and resurrection, priestly and kingship, kingdom, and rule. Note also that the proclamation of the three angels' messages is followed by the coming of the Son of man on the clouds (Rev 14:14).

Connections with the Introduction to the Seals. The good news is encapsulated in chapters 4 and 5. Life has meaning. It is related to the fact that there is a holy creator God who caused all of us to be.

In Revelation 5, the good news is in the announcement of the restoration of cosmic reconciliation and peace and worship and celebration. The Lamb is victorious. He has conquered. He was slain, and now He is standing. He died and was resurrected.

A STORY OF TRANSFORMATION

NEEDS
In chapter 5 there is crisis, a cosmic crisis, signaled by two elements in our text.

- No one is found in heaven, on earth, or under the earth, worthy to open the book or even to look at it.

- As a result, John weeps a lot.

COMPETENCE
The first issue signaled by the question "who is worthy" is that of competence. However, the nature of the competence is subtle. The qualifications of the competent one present several unexpected features and paradoxes.

He is introduced as a Lion who has conquered. However, what John sees is a Lamb as slain, but standing. The Lamb has seven horns and seven eyes. In the hymn of verses 9 and 10, several performances are cited as proof that the Lamb is qualified or worthy.

PERFORMANCES
- Victory.

- Redemption: "You . . . [have] purchased for God with Your blood men from every tribe and tongue and people and nation" (5:9).

- Creation/Re-creation (He has made us into the following:)

  a. Kingdom.
  b. Priests to our God.
  c. Kings: "They will reign upon the earth" (5:10).

RESOLUTION AND RECOGNITIONS

Revelation 5 presents several reversals. The problems that occasioned the cosmic crisis are multifaceted. The solutions are also multifaceted. This chapter portrays a number of aspects as good news.

- New song instead of the weeping.

- The prayers of the saints are answered.

- Discourse and dialogue are again possible.

- Intensification of praises (music and songs of gratitude from many angels, the living creatures, and the elders, numbering myriads of myriads and thousands of thousands).

- Acknowledgement of God's attributes.

- Cosmic doxology.

- The "Amen" is uttered as sign and seal of the covenant.

- Worship is accomplished.

The whole section of the seals shows that the good news of salvation includes the following:

- Resolution of a cosmic crisis.

- Reversal of despair.

- Restoration of God's kingdom.

- Restitution of priestly dignity and function.

- Reinstatement of kings.

- Reunion of the cosmic family.

- Resumption of worship, praises, and songs in celebration and in gratitude for the salvation fulfilled by the blood of the Lamb.

NOTE: A CRUCIAL ELEMENT OF THE GOOD NEWS

A key aspect of the good news is the restoration of justice.

- What the Lamb who was slain and standing secures is the restoration of a divine order of justice.

- "When he opened the fifth seal, I saw under the altar the souls of those who had been slain for the word of God, and for the witness they had borne; they cried out with a loud voice, 'O Sovereign Lord, holy and true, how long before thou wilt judge and avenge our blood on those who dwell on the earth?'" (6:9-10, RSV).

- "Then they were each given a white robe and told to rest a little longer, until the number of their fellow servants and their brethren should be complete, who were to be killed as they themselves had been" (6:11-RSV).

- The good news is restoration of justice.

- The good news is also expressed in chapter 7: God's people, the servants and worshipers, are sealed.

- The whole series of the seven seals then reveals several aspects of the good news. But the central work of redemption is the performance of the cosmic Goel, or redeemer.

CONNECTIONS WITH THE INTERLUDE BETWEEN THE 6TH AND 7TH TRUMPETS (REVELATION 10)

As noted earlier, chapter 10 begins with the mention of another mighty angel who cries out with a loud voice (10:1-2). Before this, the last mention of a powerful angel who proclaims with a loud voice is found in chapter 5:2. Moreover, the three angels' messages to the inhabitants of the earth also begin with the mention of another angel having an everlasting gospel to proclaim. Therefore, there is a close relationship between chapters 5, 10, and 14, which we will now explore.

PEOPLE OF PROPHETS AND MESSENGERS OF MERCY AND HOPE

From a structural, contextual, and thematic perspective, the three angels' messages occur between the sixth and the seventh trumpets as God's last attempt to bring the world back to Him before it is too late. The sixth trumpet ends with a note of regret. Despite the plagues that fall on a third of mankind, there is no repentance.

The rest of mankind, who were not killed by these plagues, did not repent of the works of their hands, so as not to worship demons, and the idols of gold and of silver and of brass and of stone and of wood, which can neither see nor hear nor walk; and they did not repent of their murders nor of their sorceries nor of their immorality nor of their thefts (Rev 9:20-21).

Twice then, the idea of lack of repentance is underlined. Nevertheless, the end of the world does not come without a time of grace, precisely to give humanity an opportunity to repent.

The three angels' messages are in essence a call to repentance and a message of restoration and hope. Even the warning aspects contained in them are ultimately driven by the love of God, who "wants all people to be saved and to come to the knowledge of the truth" (1 Tim 2:4, NASB).

The end-time context makes proclaiming the gospel as the mystery of God and the three angels' messages urgent prior to the Second Coming of Jesus Christ to heal completely all the wounds of human existence.

A NETWORK OF PARALLELS AND CONNECTIONS

The themes present in Revelation 10 and 11 are part of a network of texts in the book of Revelation, in the New Testament, and in the Old Testament. They are about the revelation of God (theophany), covenant, revelations of titles and functions of Jesus Christ, the subject and object of the Revelation: Son of man, High Priest, Lamb sacrifice and resurrection, Lion of the tribe of Judah, the One who has conquered and who rules, time elements, the proclamation of the mystery of God, the commissioning of God's people to evangelize, the eating of a book with its Old Testament parallels, and the difficulty of the mission.

These networks of thematic connections, though, should not distract us from seeing the unique perspectives of the book of Revelation. The Apostle John is not simply a repetiteur of the material found elsewhere in the Bible. Every text is unique. Making references to parallel texts is not in itself an explanation.

Nonetheless, God is consistent with His character. In the 8th century B.C., He told His prophet Amos that the Lord does not do anything without revealing His secret to His servants the prophets (Amos 3:7).

Before the end of the northern kingdom, God sent several prophets to bring Israel back to a covenant relationship with Him. He sent Amos, Hosea, Isaiah, and Micah. Likewise, before the end of the southern kingdom of Judah, God sent the prophets Zephaniah and Jeremiah to spare His people from destruction and exile. Even during national tragedy, He used prophets like Daniel and Ezekiel to woo His people back to Him.

Before the end of this world, God sends His messages, servants, and prophets to deliver a message of hope amid unavoidable judgment. The message is called the everlasting gospel. The necessity of preaching the everlasting gospel was emphasized in chapter 10, precisely between the sixth and the seventh trumpets in what is known as an interlude, a pattern of pause between the sixth and the seventh elements of the series of seals, trumpets, and plagues.

In Revelation 10, the mighty angel displays a divine dignity similar to that of the Son of man, the High Priest of chapter 1. The whole scene can be legitimately associated with Old Testament theophany settings.

The seven thunders are likely messages of judgment. The fact that John is forbidden to write their content is more in consonance with the focus on a particular mission, that of preaching the gospel before the Second Coming to give the inhabitants of the world a last invitation to return to God. The lament in the sixth trumpet, which twice noted that the inhabitants of the world did not repent, could have led to a call for executive judgment and the sounding of the seventh trumpet for the kingdom of God finally to succeed the kingdoms of the world. But instead, God demonstrates His compassion and desire to forgive by commissioning His end-time remnant people to be His messengers of mercy. These are the ones described in chapter 12 as those who keep the commandments of God and the faith of Jesus. They appear on the scene of history, a history marked by a great controversy displayed in the same chapter 12. It climaxes in the coalition of a counterfeit trinity determined to thwart God's plan to save the world. The three spirits like frogs that go all over the world to build a coalition against God's purposes and people are a counterfeit of the three angels' messages.

> And I saw coming out of the mouth of the dragon and out of the mouth of the beast and out of the mouth of the false prophet, three unclean spirits like frogs; for they are spirits of demons, performing signs, which go out to the kings of the whole world, to gather them together for the war of the great day of God, the Almighty. ("Behold, I am coming like a thief. Blessed is the one who stays awake and keep his clothes, so that he will not walk about naked and men will not see his shame.") (Rev 16:13-15)

In the text, the activities of the counterfeit of the three angels' messages take place in the final events just prior to the Second Coming of Jesus Christ (described in Rev 19:11-21). Therefore, the call to stay vigilant occurs in this same context.

THE IMMEDIATE CONTEXT OF REVELATION 14
General Observations

The immediate context shows that Revelation 14 displays a message of resistance against totalitarian and authoritarian political and religious institutions and entities. It is a pushback message against usurpers of God's unique prerogatives and against abuses of human rights (Rev 12 and 13).

The dragon and its allies, religious and political beasts, are resisted by the remnant that upholds the sovereignty of God through the keeping of God's commandments and the faith of Jesus. Jesus' substitutionary sacrifice, Jesus' victory, Jesus' righteousness—not the works or ritual performances of eccle-siastical bodies—matter when it comes to salvation. The vision of the 144,000 on Mount Zion, following the Lamb wherever He goes, sets the tone in reference to what really matters: a focus on Jesus, the One who makes standing possible, having Himself been slain but is now standing.

FOCUS ON THE TEXT

Centering on Revelation 14, the following description of its content is in order. Revelation 14 begins with the vision of the 144,000 standing with the Lamb, following the Lamb wherever He goes. They are standing on Mount Zion, the text specifies, with harps, and singing their song of experience.

Another vision of a group with similar characteristics (Rev 15:2-4) seems to provide an inclusio to this section. It climaxes with the vision of a group of victors again standing, this time beside the sea of glass, with harps and singing the song of Moses the servant of God and the song of the Lamb who we were told was slain but standing.

These visions of victors are the most fascinating part of the whole section. It is all about celebration of victory, festivity, and joy, and exalting of God who made their victory possible.

We were already told in Revelation 12:10-12 in a celebratory mode that

Now the salvation, and the power, and the kingdom of our God and the authority of His Christ have come, for the accuser of our brethren has been thrown down, he who accuses them before our God day and night. And they overcame him [Satan] because of the blood of the Lamb and the word of their testimony, and they did not love their life even when faced with death. For this reason, rejoice, O heavens and you who dwell in them. Woe to the earth and the sea, because the devil has come down to you, having great wrath, knowing that he has only a short time.

In Revelation 14, the celebration—the glorification—of the victory is described. It is about music and singing. One of the fascinating ways to engage how the book of Revelation makes its meaning is to follow the music, the singing, the praise, and the exuberant joy which spring from various scenes throughout the book. In scholarly language, this means identifying the hymnic material. The hymns provide the reader with rhetorical indications of the persuasion strategies of the writer. These hymns function as invitations to adopt the values that the writer upholds throughout the book. The attempt to create a desire to join the festivities functions as an exhortation (parenesis) to embrace God's sovereignty and to be faithful to God's purposes regardless of the circumstances. The description of the 144,000 as the introductory scene to the three angels' messages is also parenetic in nature. It displays what is desired. The characteristics associated with the 144,000 are what is desired for God's victorious people: redeemed from the earth, not defiling themselves, exclusive allegiance to the Lamb, no lie found in their mouths, and blameless (Rev 14:3-5).

We may not readily see these aspects of the text because of the different questions we may be asking of the text, almost exclusively questions related to the fulfillment of end-time prophecies.

What if we ask the text what the questions are that it asks? Then it becomes easier to enter the world of the text. In the setting of the seven seals, the text asks four questions that lead to a better grasp on the issues in this series:

- 1. Who is worthy? (5:2)

- 2. How long? [Until when?] (6:10)

- 3. Who will be able to stand? (6:17)

- 4. Who are these, and where do they come from? (7:13)

These questions the text of Revelation asked and clearly provided answers. Revelation 14 and 15 give us crucial insights into the development of the story of the whole book.

Revelation 14 and 15 provide us with the climax of the story of the book of Revelation, the ultimate good news. It is certainly about end time, not tribulations but rather jubilation, end-time jubilation, singing, playing of music, celebration, song of freedom, song of Exodus, song of Moses, but more, the song of the Lamb slain but standing. This is the most profound message of hope displayed in this section. God invites us to join the eschatological festival of joy, of gratitude for being saved from the powers hostile to God's reign, kingdom, and rule.

From this perspective, the closing of the book also reiterates what really matters, which is being invited to the marriage supper of the Lamb (Rev 19:9). This is one of the seven beatitudes, or blessings, in the book of Revelation.

As we share the end-time message, we must not overlook the climax in the joyful celebration of the redeemed, the climactic music, and the chorus singing the victory of God.

That is the climax of the covenant.

However, the heart of the covenant is Jesus Christ. The book is about the revelation of Jesus Christ. At its deepest level, the good news is God's self-revelation in Jesus Christ.

He is revealed as Jesus Christ, the one who loves us and delivered us from our sins and made us into a kingdom of priests. He is also revealed as the Son of man, the representative of humanity, the High Priest amid the seven lampstands, which represent the churches. He is also revealed as the Lamb as if slain but standing, but also as the Shepherd who leads God's redeemed people into the springs of the water of life (Rev 7:17). He is also the one who commissioned God's people to preach the mystery of God (the gospel) before the sounding of the seventh trumpet, just prior to the advent of God's kingdom when it will be said:

"'The kingdom of the world has become the kingdom of our Lord and of His Christ; and He will reign forever and ever'" (Rev 11:15).

CHAPTER 20

THE THREE ANGELS' MESSAGES: THE CONTENT

Ganoune Diop

The three angels' messages contain certain vital aspects:

- An Invitation.

- A Prophetic Pronouncement.

- A Warning.

- An Appeal to Perseverance in keeping God's commandments and having faith in Jesus Christ.

- A Blessing pronounced by the Holy Spirit for those who die in the Lord.

The three angels' messages are a profound condensed summary of major biblical motifs: the eternal gospel, divine sovereignty, creation, judgment, salvation, worship, glorification of God, justification of those who have faith in Jesus, righteousness by faith, the kingdom of God, and everlasting fellowship.

In its most profound and comprehensive nature, the gospel is God's self-revelation, manifested through His multifaceted acts of salvation.

The good news is God's self-revelation in Jesus Christ. This in fact is the very title of the book: The Revelation of Jesus Christ.

Jesus is the prophet, but more than a prophet. He is the Word of God incarnate. He is the once-and-for-all sacrifice, the Lamb of God who solved the problem of the world. He is King of kings, Lord of lords, the Lion of the tribe of Judah, destined to rule the whole universe.

THE FIRST ANGEL'S MESSAGE

THE MEANING OF THE FEAR OF LORD

On the one hand the Bible says, "Fear not." On the other the Bible says, "Fear." This shows that the word fear is characterized by polysemy—it can signify different referents.

ILLUSTRATION: THE FEAR OF THE LORD IN PROVERBS

There is a rich history of usage for the expression "fear of the Lord" in the Bible. For example, the Book of Proverbs provides us with various connotations for this expression, attaching several nuances to the concept of the "fear of the Lord."[1]

---

[1] Following is a list of the "fear of the Lord" passages in Proverbs (New American Standard Bible, 1995 edition, here and throughout):

1. Proverbs 1:7 The fear of the LORD is the beginning of knowledge; fools despise wisdom and instruction.

2. Proverbs 1:29 Because they hated knowledge and did not choose the fear of the LORD.

3. Proverbs 2:1-6 My son, if you will receive my words, and treasure my commandments within you, 2 make your ear attentive to wisdom, incline your heart to understanding; 3 for if you cry for discernment, lift your voice for understanding; 4 if you seek her as silver, and search for her as for hidden treasures; 5 then you will discern the fear of the LORD and discover the knowledge of God. 6 For the LORD gives wisdom; from His mouth come knowledge and understanding.

4. Proverbs 3:7 Do not be wise in your own eyes; fear the LORD and turn away from evil.

5. Proverbs 8:13 "The fear of the LORD is to hate evil; pride and arrogance and the evil way and the perverted mouth, I hate."

6. Proverbs 9:10 The fear of the LORD is the beginning of wisdom, and the knowledge of the Holy One is understanding.

7. Proverbs 10:27 The fear of the LORD prolongs life, but the years of the wicked will be shortened.

8. Proverbs 14:2 He who walks in his uprightness fears the LORD, but he who is devious in his ways despises Him.

9. Proverbs 14:26 In the fear of the LORD there is strong confidence, and his children will have refuge.

10. Proverbs 14:27 The fear of the LORD is a fountain of life, that one may avoid the snares of death.

11. Proverbs 15:16 Better is a little with the fear of the LORD than great treasure and turmoil with it.

12. Proverbs 15:33 The fear of the LORD is the instruction for wisdom, and before honor comes humility.

13. Proverbs 16:6-9 By lovingkindness and truth iniquity is atoned for, and by the fear of the LORD one keeps away from evil. 7 When a man's ways are pleasing to the LORD, He makes even his enemies to be at peace with him. 8 Better is a little with righteousness than great income with injustice. 9 The mind of man plans his way, But the LORD directs his steps.

14. Proverbs 19:23 The fear of the LORD leads to life, so that one may sleep satisfied, untouched by evil.

15. Proverbs 22:4 The reward of humility and the fear of the LORD are riches, honor and life.

A comprehensive view of the fear of the Lord in the book of Proverbs can be expressed as follows:

- To know the Holy One.

- To enter the path of wisdom.

- To love life and to choose the path that leads to life.

- To trust in the Lord.

- To treasure God's commandments.

- To discern righteousness and justice and equity and every good course.

- To hate and shun all evil.

- To avoid the snares of death.

- To be humble, dissociating oneself from pride, arrogance, and abuse (perverted speech).

- To develop an attitude of contentment.

In the Book of Proverbs, the fear of the Lord is therefore an existential attitude, a resolve to depend on the God of life, to acknowledge His holiness, giving heed to His wisdom, and walking in the path of life accordingly.

In the context of Revelation 14, to fear God is primarily to desist from idolatry and to devote oneself to a life of glorifying God and worshiping Him alone. The angel who appeared to the Apostle John reminded him of this important aspect (Rev 19:10).

In the setting of Revelation 14, the fear of God implies the following:

---

16. Proverbs 23:17-18 Do not let your heart envy sinners, but live in the fear of the LORD always. 18 Surely there is a future, and your hope will not be cut off.

17. Proverbs 24:21 My son, fear the LORD and the king; do not associate with those who are given to change.

18. Proverbs 29:25 The fear of man brings a snare, but he who trusts in the LORD will be exalted.

19. Proverbs 31:30 Charm is deceitful, and beauty is vain, but a woman who fears the LORD, she shall be praised.

- Total dedication to God, an allegiance undeterred by the threat of God's enemies.

- Awareness of God's constant presence.

- Renunciation and avoidance of evil and sin.

- Repentance and renunciation of usurping God's glory.

- Ascription of all worth to God, which is the essence of worship.

- Remembrance of God's justice and judgment.

- Expectation of the Second Coming.

- A life of gratitude because of the gift of justification by faith and imputed righteousness.

- Rest, peace.

- A life centered on God the Father, Son, and Holy Spirit.

CONTENT OF THE FIRST ANGEL'S MESSAGE

In essence, the first angel's message calls for freedom from idolatry. Only God is the creator. God is the only one worthy to be worshiped and glorified.

The first angel's message is also an invitation to life, to awareness of God, being mindful of God, constantly living in the presence of God, which is the equivalent of piety.

We are invited to a life of affirmation of God's sovereignty, God's rights. We give God all the glory in all gratitude for His being the creator, the judge, and the redeemer. The expression "Fear God" essentially is an invitation to affirm the sovereignty of God, the God of life.

THE SECOND ANGEL'S MESSAGE

The second angel's message is about freedom and the end of exile, freedom from oppression. It is freedom from the rule of totalitarian regimes, whether political or religious freedom from the message and miracles of Babylon.

When God's people were told that Babylon had fallen, they understood that it was time for the Exodus, a homecoming, and a reunion. It was indeed the advent of freedom. It is the good news of going home at last. In both the old and new covenant, the fall of Babylon is good news of freedom from captivity. The reason why the fall of Babylon is good news is elucidated further in Revelation 17. Not only is Babylon the hub of immorality and blasphemy, but Babylon is depicted as "drunk with the blood of the saints, and with the blood of the witnesses of Jesus" (v. 6). As such, the fall of Babylon is an act of justice from God. It is also an answer to the cry for justice expressed in the fifth seal. Those under the altar, who have had their lives sacrificed, asked God, "How long, O Lord, holy and true, will you refrain from judging and avenging our blood on those who dwell on the earth?" (Rev 6:10).

THE THIRD ANGEL'S MESSAGE

The third angel's message is an invitation to choose, based on freedom. It also contains a warning about the consequences of our existential choice. It is furthermore an invitation to embrace the righteousness of God. It offers freedom from human-made substitutes for the real salvation offered by the only Savior, Jesus Christ. This is freedom from defilement, freedom from siding with the powers that are hostile to God's sovereignty.

The third angel's message is an appeal to absolute dedication to God, a commitment to unswerving allegiance to God. It is the positive side of freedom—freedom to fellowship with God. This message was already signified in the introductory vision of the chapter, the vision of the 144,000 who follow the Lamb wherever He goes. They have Jesus' name and the name of His Father written on their foreheads (Rev 14:1).

CALL TO FREEDOM:
In the context of the three angels' messages, the gospel is the following:

- Freedom from idolatry.

- Freedom from captivity in Egypt and Babylon.

- Freedom from sharing the fate of God's enemy, avoiding total annihilation.

The core message that we share is about Jesus Christ—God's self-revelation in Jesus Christ, to be specific. After all, this is the title of the Book of Revelation, the purpose of the whole book. Jesus Christ, as the Gospels were meant to show, is God's beloved Son in whom God is entirely pleased. He is the "radiance of [God's] glory and the exact representation of His nature," according to the Book of Hebrews (Heb 1:3).

JESUS AND THE THREE ANGELS' MESSAGES

Jesus embodies the three angels' messages. Ellen White expressed this truth this way:

> Of all professing Christians, Seventh-day Adventists should be foremost in uplifting Christ before the world. The proclamation of the third angel's message calls for the presentation of the Sabbath truth. This truth, with others included in this message, is to be proclaimed; **but the great center of attraction, Christ Jesus**, must not be left out.[2]

Furthermore, Jesus proclaimed every element of the three angels' messages. "Fear God," "Give Him glory," and "Worship God" are three motifs at the heart of Jesus' life and teachings.

The temptations Jesus faced find their parallels in the three Angels messages

- In essence, the fear of the Lord is associated with being blessed.

- The teachings of Jesus in the beatitudes are the gospel condensed.[3]

- The call to fear the Lord is a call to avail oneself of God's blessings.

---

[2] Ellen G. White, *Gospel Workers* (Washington, DC: Review and Herald, 1915), 156, emphasis supplied.

[3] Frederick Dale Bruner, *The Christbook: Matthew 1-12*, revised and expanded edition (Grand Rapids, MI: Eerdmans, 2007), 157-182.

- The ones who fear the Lord are:

  - The poor in spirit who depend on God.

  - Those who mourn and rely on God's comfort.

  - The meek who wait on the Lord.

  - Those who hunger and thirst for righteousness.

  - The merciful.

  - The pure in heart.

  - The peace makers.

  - Those who are persecuted for righteousness' sake.

Those who fear the Lord depend on God. They wait on God. They are Adventists, not just waiting for the Second Coming but waiting on the Lord in everything.

The blessings that are graced to those who fear the Lord are the following:

- Theirs is the kingdom.

- They shall be comforted.

- They shall inherit the earth.

- They shall be satisfied or filled.

- They shall obtain mercy.

- They shall see God.

- They shall be called sons of God.

The climax of all blessings is to see God face to face. This is the supreme good.

- This blessing *par excellence* creates a fascination and a heartfelt gratitude, both of which trigger genuine worship.

- Unhindered everlasting fellowship will finally become reality.

- God will dwell among His people in a new environment: a new heaven and a new earth.

God's original purpose to bless human beings and creation will finally be fulfilled: "There will no longer be any curse" (Rev 22:3). The first act of God after creating living creatures is to bless them (Gen 1:22). God's first act after the creation of Adam and Eve was to bless them (Gen 1:28).

At the Second Coming, all traces of curse will be completely removed. The pervading advent of blessing will bring a new cosmic world order. Jesus will have succeeded in restoring the blessing God intended for the whole world.

The important aspect of the Christian message is the acknowledgment that while the reality of seeing God face to face is yet to come, it is already available from the One who is the face of God. "He who has seen Me has seen the Father" (John 14:9).

At the deeper level,

- The beatitudes are a veiled portrait of Jesus Christ himself.

- Jesus epitomizes God's kingdom and righteousness, presence, and fellowship.

The second element in the first angel's message, "give glory to Him," also resonates with Jesus' life and teachings:

- Jesus lived to glorify God the Father, as stated in John 17 at the end of His mission on earth.

- In the setting of the Sermon on the Mount, He admonishes His followers—those who are the salt and light of the world —to do good deeds so that others may glorify the Father.

- To give God the glory is to live a life of truth. It is developing an ever-present consciousness of God's sovereignty and grace. All good comes from God.

- To live truthfully implies a resolve not to usurp God's prerogatives.

- To give God the glory develops an attitude of gratitude. The prerequisite for this attitude is humility.

- The third element of the first angel's message is also a key element of Jesus' life and teachings. He taught us to refuse to worship the devil and to be committed to worship God alone.

WORSHIP

The overarching motif of the three angels' messages can be summed up by means of the concept of worship. In the setting of this chapter, worship is:

- An expression of the covenant of grace (worshipers celebrate God's role as creator and His judgment/justice, triumph, and care).

- A response to God's mighty acts of redemption and liberation (the 144,000 are redeemed).

- Prompted by the proclamation of the everlasting gospel, worship is celebration of the good news.

- It is an awe-inspiring experience, leading to repentance ("Fear God").

- It is complete devotion to God's character, prerogatives, and purposes.

- It is honoring, revering, and acknowledging God's holiness.

- Worship is glorification and vindication of God's name.

- It is kingdom centered (Babylon is fallen).

- It is joyful (a new song, the song of Moses and the Lamb, a song that stems from a unique experience of being delivered by God).

- It is experiential encounter, personal response to God's redemptive acts in our lives and in the world through the victorious Lamb and the Holy Spirit.

- Worship is enactment of our condition of belonging to God.

- It is total dedication to following Jesus wherever He goes (disciples are the true worshipers of God). Worship is a lifestyle of walking with God.

- It is Spirit-tuned, Spirit-led, and Spirit-filled.

- It is availing oneself to receive the assurance of grace.

- It is affirmation of our desire to be sealed by God.

- It is living out values that are holy and counter-cultural, rejecting those values that are foreign or opposite to God's sovereignty and kingdom.

- Worship is God-centered (it is about God).

- It is a symbol of our submission and surrender of will to God's supreme purpose in creating us.

- It is a sign of an end-time covenant in the setting of the great controversy between God and His remnant church determined to keep His commandments and the faith of Jesus on the one hand, and on the other, Satan and his rebellious angels and his earthly allies, whether religious or political.

- Worship is an expression of our desire for the Second Coming.

- It is an anticipation and foretaste of heaven.

- Worship is a choice to receive and to live by the revelation of God's attributes.

- Worship is a declaration that all glory goes to God: *Soli Deo Gloria.*

SUMMARY OF INSIGHTS INTO WORSHIP

- To worship God is to express one's love, gratitude, and devotion to God for God's sake. Worship therefore involves fearing God, giving Him glory, and worshiping Him alone. The outcome of worship is to devote oneself completely and constantly to remembering, affirming, and testifying to God's sovereignty and bountiful grace.

- To worship God is to contemplate God's beauty—the beauty of His mighty acts of deliverance, judgment, and justice.

- To worship is to express one's soul-stirring gratitude for the unmerited favor of God's grace. God welcomes sinners and eats with them! Worship contains therefore an inseparable element of fellowship.

- The worshiper does not come to God divided. His whole being is a sacrifice to God.

- The whole Old Testament sacrificial system prefigured not only the sacrifice of Christ, which is the centerpiece, but also a lifestyle of sacrificial living, since only a holy person can be pleasing to God.

- In a nutshell, to worship God is to ascribe to God supreme worth. Discipleship is the logical development of such existential disposition.

- A person who truly worships God is healed from the idolatry of considering anything or anybody else to be worthy of his devotion, praise, or prayer.

- True worship is therefore liberating. Things and people remain in their assigned place in the created order. Reality is viewed from a God-centered perspective that is also a Christocentric and Spirit-centric perspective.

SUMMARY

Revelation 14 has multifaceted information that needs careful delineation.

1. The proclamation of an eternal gospel or good news.

2. An invitation to life, to be mindful of God the creator.

3. A call to God's vindication, that is, to giving God all the glory.

4. An imperative to worship God in truth and in all gratitude.

5. A prophetic pronouncement of the defeat of the oppressors of God's people. Babylon is fallen. When in ancient times God's people were told that Babylon is fallen, it meant the end of captivity and consequently that God's people could go home.

6. A warning not to share the fate of the counterfeit Lamb.

7. An encouragement to persevere in honoring God through obedience to God's commandments.

8. A call to perseverance in the faith of Jesus, regardless of end-time circumstances. Jesus Christ is our sufficiency.

9. An assurance of blessing for those who die in the Lord, whether martyrs or those who die a natural death as believers in Jesus Christ.

10. The certainty that the hour of the harvest will come, just as the hour of judgment has come. The former is about the saved, while the latter is about those who have rejected God's gospel of salvation.

11. The Second Coming is described right after the three angels' messages. It is part of the essence of the good news. It speaks about the coming of the Savior who will finally deliver the world from evil and establish God's everlasting kingdom.

12. This section of the Book of Revelation climaxes in the celebration of the redeemed standing beside the sea of glass, playing music and singing their songs of gratitude to God—songs of deliverance, the song of Moses and the song of unfathomable love, the song of the Lamb.

In conclusion, the three angels' messages are about God's sovereignty and Christ's sufficiency, already signified in the determination of the 144,000 to follow the Lamb wherever He goes. They are loyal to Christ, who is our sufficiency. The inaugural vision of the 144,000 surely indicates that God's loyal people find in Jesus Christ all that they need. They will not consent to allow His unique prerogatives to be usurped. The counterfeit trinity of Revelation 13, oppressors of God's people, trying to impose their world order through coercion, are resisted by the Remnant who keep the commandments of God and the faith of Jesus. They are a resistant movement. They are signs of God's sovereignty. There are people on earth prior to the Second Coming whose supreme and only allegiance is to Jesus Christ.

God's end-time people are characterized by the act of listening to the voice of the Holy Spirit. They have responded to the voice of the Holy Spirit. "He who has an ear, let him what the Spirit says to the churches" (Rev 2:7, 11, 17, 29; 3:6, 13, 22). These are seven exhortations to listen to the Spirit. The other important theme in the letters to the seven churches, which is also found in the climax of Revelation 14, is that of overcoming.

The content of Revelation 14 and 15 is indeed the restoration of the true Trinity: the sovereignty of God the Father, the sufficiency of Christ's provision for salvation, and the comforting and sanctifying presence of the Holy Spirit.

The Spirit pronounced a blessing on those who die in the Lord, whether through being martyred or through natural death. Jesus had promised that the second death will have no power over those who trust in Him.

May we not forget that our message is about uplifting the victorious Lamb, the one who knew no sin but who became sin so that we might have the righteousness of God through Him who "became to us wisdom from God, and righteousness and sanctification, and redemption, so that, just as it is written, 'LET HIM WHO BOAST, BOAST IN THE LORD'" (1 Cor 1:30).

The main content of Revelation 14 is about the Lamb of God, slain but standing. He is the one prophesied in the first chapters of the Bible, the first gospel or protoevangelium, the announcement of the coming of the one who will defeat the serpent and deliver those held captive, those oppressed, those persecuted for righteousness' sake, for Jesus' sake. Jesus is indeed the righteousness of God. As the Apostle Paul puts it, Jesus is the one "who is our hope" (1 Tim 1:1). This hope joins our faith and love of God.

Jesus is the One we uplift before the world, so that the world may be drawn to Him for an eternal life of fellowship in love.

The true issue about the great controversy was about the love of God, which Lucifer and a third of the angels doubted. He continues the same scheme to make humans have doubt about the love of God.

Jesus came as a demonstration that "'God so loved the world that He gave His unique Son, that whoever believes in Him shall not perish, but have eternal life'" (John 3:16, margin). The end of the great controversy is significantly described in the following words:

The great controversy is ended. Sin and sinners are no more. The entire universe is clean. One pulse of harmony and gladness beats through the vast creation. From Him who created all, flow life and light and gladness, throughout the realms of illimitable space. From the minutest atom to the greatest world, all things, animate and inanimate, in their unshadowed beauty and perfect joy, declare that God is love.[4]

That was the real issue all along—the love of God doubted, and the love of God demonstrated.

After all, the last message to be given to the world is about the love of God. As Ellen White stated:

The last message of mercy to be given to the world, is a revelation of His character of love. The children of God are to manifest His glory. In their own life and character they are to reveal what the grace of God has done for them.[5]

This is what we share with the world for the vindication of God and for the salvation of as many as possible. For God wants all people to be saved and to come to the knowledge of the truth (1 Tim 2:3-4).

We invite the world to join the upcoming festival of joy, the independence of independences, the ultimate celebration of liberation and the freedom to join the singing and the playing of music as an expression of the deepest gratitude of our souls. After all, music is the language of the soul. The redeemed people will be engaged in unprecedented praise and worship of God, who is love.

[4] Ellen G. White, *The Great Controversy* (Mountain View, CA: Pacific Press, 1911), 678.

[5] Ellen G. White, *Christ's Object Lessons* (Washington, DC: Review and Herald, 1900), 415-416.

CHAPTER 21

THE ETERNAL GOSPEL IN THE BOOK OF REVELATION

Ganoune Diop

Here is a critical question: Is the gospel in Revelation different from the gospel in the rest of the New Testament? More specifically, is the eternal gospel of the first angel's message in Revelation 14:6 different from what the Apostle Paul fiercely defended as the unchangeable and irreplaceable gospel? He said that even if an angel should come with another gospel, let him be anathema. For Paul the content of the gospel was non-negotiable.

> I am amazed that you are so quickly deserting Him who called you by the grace of Christ, for a different gospel; which is really not another; only there are some who are disturbing you and want to distort the gospel of Christ. But even if we, or an angel from heaven, should preach to you a gospel contrary to what we have preached to you, he is to be accursed! As we have said before, so I say again now, if any man is preaching to you a gospel contrary to what you received, he is to be accursed! (Gal 1:6-8)[1]

Contextually, the use of the expression "eternal gospel" may be a corrective to a counterfeit gospel. Revelation 13 describes a counterfeit trinity with its counterfeit gospel of works, deception, and coercion.

In this context, the three angels' messages are a work of restoration. The eternal gospel must be restored, pointing as it

---

[1] Unless otherwise noted, Scripture quotations are from the New American Standard Bible, 1995 edition.

does to the sovereignty of God the creator of all reality and, as an angel later reminds John (Rev 19:10), the only one to whom all glory must be ascribed and the only one worthy to be worshiped.

It has been stated that

> The 'everlasting gospel' in the end-times restores the New Testament gospel in its wholeness, in its integrity. It explains God's plan to save men and women in such a way that their presence in the new earth would not jeopardize again the well-being and security of the universe.[2]

However, even though this gospel is not different from the good news one consistently finds in the Bible, there is more to the holistic everlasting gospel from a biblical perspective.

As such, from the protoevangelium or first gospel of Genesis 3:15 to the eternal gospel, there seems to be a variety of meanings, with subtle nuances to delineate.

Key Insight:

> At its most profound and comprehensive nature, the gospel is God's self-revelation in Jesus Christ through the Holy Spirit, manifested through God's multifaceted acts of salvation, based on His love and absolute purpose to fellowship with the redeemed throughout ceaseless ages.

The good news is Jesus Christ, God's self-revelation. This aspect is intimated by the very title of the book: The Revelation of Jesus Christ. He is the prophet, but more than a prophet— He is the Word of God incarnate. He is the Lamb of God, God's sacrifice, the once-and-for-all sacrifice, who solves the problems of the world. He is the One in the midst of the throne. He is King of kings, Lord of lords, the Lion of the tribe of Judah, destined to rule the whole universe.

This understanding of Jesus as the gospel is consonant with what is revealed in the New Testament.

---

[2] Herbert E. Douglas, "What is the 'Everlasting Gospel'?" *Journal of the Adventist Theological Society*, 12/2 (Spring 2001), 150.

THE GOSPEL THAT JESUS AND THE APOSTLES PREACHED

1. Jesus said, the gospel of the kingdom will be preached to the whole world and then the end shall come (Matt 24:14). This is the gospel the Apostle Paul preached, up to the day he died in Rome. After clearly telling the Jews that "the salvation of God has been sent to the Gentiles, and they will hear it," Paul continued to preach Christ to everyone:

> Paul dwelt two whole years in his own rented house, and received all who came to him, preaching the kingdom of God and teaching the things which concern the Lord Jesus Christ with all confidence. (Acts 28:28, 30-31, NKJV)

2. Jesus spoke about the gospel in many ways. One of His famous ways of defining the gospel is in His parables. One can, for example, understand the gospel to be about **God's hospitality, pictured in the father's welcoming generosity** to the prodigal son (Luke 15). The parable gives a clear message that God is interested in saving lives, in **forgiving His children and restoring their dignity.**

3. The gospel is the power of God for salvation. "For I am not ashamed of the gospel, for it is the power of God for salvation to everyone who believes, to the Jew first and also to the Greek. For in it the righteousness of God is revealed from faith for faith, as it is written, "The righteous shall live by faith" (Rom 1:16-17, ESV).

4. The gospel is the good news that God has cancelled the condemnation that hovers over the whole human family because of sin. As the Apostle Paul puts it in Romans 8:1: "There is therefore now no condemnation for those who are in Christ Jesus" (ESV). We are delivered from the penalty of sin and from the power of sin (Rom 6:14). And soon, at the Second Coming, we will be delivered from the very presence of sin. That is part of the blessed hope.

5. The gospel is the good news that the death and resurrection of Jesus provide salvation for those who believe in Him. No other gospel came from the lips or pen of the Apostle Paul.

Now I make known to you, brethren, the gospel which I preached to you, which also you received, in which also you stand, by which also you are saved, if you hold fast the word which I preached to you, unless you believed in vain.

For I delivered to you as of first importance what I also received, that Christ died for our sins according to the Scriptures, and that He was buried, and that He was raised on the third day according to the Scriptures, and that He appeared to Cephas, then to the twelve. After that He appeared to more than five hundred brethren at one time, most of whom remain until now, but some have fallen asleep. (1 Cor 15:1-6)

6. The gospel is atonement through Christ. The gospel of substitution and reconciliation features prominently in the Apostle Paul's proclamation. In 2 Corinthians 5:20-21, he says,

We are ambassadors for Christ, as though God were making an appeal through us; we beg you on behalf of Christ, be reconciled to God. He made Him who knew no sin to be sin on our behalf, so that we might become the righteousness of God in Him.

A cosmic perspective on this concept of reconciliation is articulated in Colossians 1:19-20. "It was the Father's good pleasure for all the fullness to dwell in Him, and through Him to reconcile all things to Himself, having made peace through the blood of His cross; through him, I say, whether things on earth or things in heaven."

Another significant aspect of the gospel present not only in Paul's writings but also in the Gospels is the idea of recapitulation. In this perspective, Jesus relived the history of humankind, the history of God's people.

- Jesus is the New Adam.

- Jesus is the New Moses.

- Jesus is the New Joshua.

- Jesus is the New Israel.

- Jesus embraces the destiny of the whole human family.

7. The gospel is the glory of God in the face of Jesus Christ. The Apostle Paul had emphasized this definition of the gospel in 2 Corinthians 4:3-6:

> If our gospel is veiled, it is veiled to those who are perishing, in whose case the god of this world has blinded the minds of the unbelieving so that they might not see the light of the gospel of the glory of Christ, who is the image of God. For we do not preach ourselves but Christ Jesus as Lord, and ourselves as your bond-servants for Jesus' sake. For God, who said, "Light shall shine out of darkness," is the One who has shone in our hearts to give the Light of the knowledge of the glory of God in the face of Christ.

8. The gospel is the good news of the love of God. Expanding our scope beyond Paul to the Apostle John, we find in the Johannine literature both in the Gospel of John and in the Epistles that the gospel is inseparably connected to the love of God.

- John 3:16 comes to mind, "God so loved the world, that he gave his only Son, that whoever believes in him should not perish but have eternal life" (ESV), but also verses from 1 John 4:

- "Beloved, let us love one another, for love is from God; and everyone who loves is born of God and knows God.

- "The one who does not love does not know God, for God is love. By this the love of God was manifested in us, that God has sent His only begotten Son into the world so that we might live through Him. In this is love, not that we loved God, but that He loved us and sent His Son to be the propitiation for our sins. Beloved, if God so loved us, we also ought to love one another" (1 John 4:7-11).

- The gospel is the love of God, God's benevolent disposition to save the world that He loves. The love of God was demonstrated when He sent God the Son to save the world.

- The foundation, context, and climax of the biblical revelation is that "God is love" (1 John 4:8).

Regarding this revelation, it is significant to realize that the core issue in the great controversy is the fact that Satan sowed seeds of doubt regarding the love of God. When the great controversy is over, the love of God will be recognized universally again.

9. The gospel is the good news of the New Covenant. The promise and the advent of the new covenant are integral parts of the gospel or good news. An exposition of the book of Hebrews yields fascinating insights into the gospel. The emphasis on the greater and better nature and content of the new covenant reveals the unsurpassable and incomparable greatness of Jesus Christ's prophethood, unique sacrifice, and new covenant high priestly dignity. This is the core reason why for Seventh-day Adventists, Jesus is our sufficiency. While we respect other human beings, they cannot take the place of Jesus Christ in our minds and hearts. Jesus is our sufficiency, the only mediator between God and humans, the only sacrifice, the only High Priest, the only Lord and universal King.

10. The gospel is the announcement of the good news of Jesus Christ's sufficiency for all our needs. As the Apostle Paul put it, Jesus "became to us wisdom from God, righteousness and sanctification and redemption, so that, as it is written, 'Let the one who boasts, boast in the Lord'" (1 Cor 1:30-31, ESV). Jesus Christ is our sufficiency in regard to our need for atonement, mediation, or a ruler. He is our King.

Furthermore, the Apostle Paul tells us that all the promises of God are yes in Him.

"For as many as are the promises of God, in Him they are yes; therefore also through Him is our Amen to the glory of God through us" (2 Cor 1:20).

Jesus Christ is thus the mediator *par excellence.*

11. The gospel is the good news of our adoption as children of God. There is no greater dignity than being called children of God. In Christ, argues the Apostle Paul, we are all children of God (Gal 3:26). The gospel of God specifies concerning Jesus Christ that "as many as received Him, to them He gave the right to become children of God" (John 1:12).

The theme of adoption is a significant and essential part of the good news. Ellen White highlighted this aspect of the good news:

> Through the wonderful condescension of God in our behalf, we are entitled to peculiar dignity and honor. To what greater honor could we aspire than to be called the children of God? What greater rank could we hold, what greater inheritance could we find, than that which comes to those who are heirs of God and joint heirs with Christ? "But ye are a chosen generation, a royal priesthood, a holy nation, a peculiar people; that ye should show forth the praises of him who hath called you out of darkness into his marvelous light: which in time past were not a people, but are now the people of God: which had not obtained mercy, but now have obtained mercy."[3]

12. The gospel is the good news of God's blessings. In Ephesians 1:3-14 the Apostle Paul bursts with what may be the longest sentence in the Bible—what has been called a 202-word avalanche of praise, without pause or punctuation: [4]

> Blessed be the God and Father of our Lord Jesus Christ, who has blessed us with every spiritual blessing in the heavenly places in Christ, just as He chose us in Him before the foundation of the world, that we would be holy and blameless before Him. In love He predestined us to adoption as sons through Jesus Christ to Himself, according to the kind intention of His will, to the praise of the glory of His grace, which He freely bestowed on us in the Beloved. In Him we have redemption through His

---

[3] Ellen G. White, "Words to the Young," *The Youth's Instructor*, December 8, 1892.

[4] Fred Sanders, *Embracing the Trinity: Life with God in the Gospel* (Wheaton, IL: InterVarsity, 2010), 99.

blood, the forgiveness of our trespasses, according to the riches of His grace which He lavished on us. In all wisdom and insight He made known to us the mystery of His will, according to His kind intention which He purposed in Him with a view to an administration suitable to the fullness of the times, that is, the summing up of all things in Christ, things in the heavens and things on the earth.

In Him also we have obtained an inheritance, having been predestined according to His purpose who works all things after the counsel of His will, to the end that we who were the first to hope in Christ would be to the praise of His glory. In Him, you also, after listening to the message of truth, the gospel of your salvation—having also believed, you were sealed in Him with the Holy Spirit of promise, who is given as a pledge of our inheritance, with a view to the redemption of God's own possession, to the praise of His glory.

In this context, Paul qualifies the gospel as **"the message of truth"** and **"the good news of your salvation"** (v. 13).

The blessings signified in the gospel or good news were also the climax of the Israelites' festivals, especially the day of atonement when the high priest came out and blessed the people who made it through the judgment of the day of atonement. They could therefore joyfully enter the feast of tabernacles.

Already, we are blessed with every spiritual blessing, says the Apostle Paul, but when Jesus comes again there will be the most important words pronounced as a bridge into eternity:

"'Come, you who are blessed of My Father, inherit the kingdom prepared for you from the foundation of the world'" (Matt 25:34).

13. The gospel of pcacc. In the context of defining the full armor of God necessary in the great controversy and for the purpose of standing against the schemes of the devil, the Apostle Paul subverted the military language by qualifying the gospel as the good news of peace. He further said that our struggle is not against flesh and blood, but against spiritual forces of this darkness, against the spiritual forces of wickedness in the heavenly places. He continued,

Therefore, take up the full armor of God, so that you will be able to resist in the evil day, and having done everything, to stand firm. Stand firm therefore, having GIRDED YOUR LOINS WITH TRUTH, and HAVING PUT ON THE BREASTPLATE OF RIGHTEOUSNESS, and having SHOD YOUR FEET WITH THE PREPARATION OF THE GOSPEL OF PEACE; in addition to all, taking up the shield of faith with which you will be able to extinguish all the flaming arrows of the evil one. And take THE HELMET OF SALVATION, and the sword of the Spirit, which is the word of God. (Eph 6:10-17)

Along the same line of spiritual warfare, fundamentally, the gospel is the deliverance of humanity from evil, from occupation, from the invasion of evil spirits who transformed planet earth into an occupied territory. It has been revealed that one third of the angels were expelled from heaven to earth (Rev 12:3-4). Revelation 16:14 specifies that spirits of demons go around the world to create antagonism against God and God's people.

The one who delivers the world and transforms it again into God's kingdom is Jesus Christ the Savior.

According to 2 Thessalonians 2:8, it is at the Second Coming that Jesus will defeat Satan and his allies.

14. Overall the gospel is about the advent of a Savior. The First Advent of a Savior was celebrated by angels and shepherds, and by Simeon and others.

The Second Advent will be a more glorious cosmic celebration. We will be part of this one. It will be a festival of joy, reunion, and celebration of God face to face.

15. The gospel is the good of the liberation of the whole creation. The gospel also has an ecological dimension. As the Apostle Paul put it,

For the anxious longing of the creation waits eagerly for the revealing of the sons of God. For the creation was subjected to futility, not willingly, but because of Him who subjected it, in hope that the creation itself also will be set free from its slavery to corruption into the freedom of the glory of the children of God. For we know that the whole creation groans and suffers the pains of childbirth together until now. And not only this, but also we ourselves, having the first fruits of the Spirit, even we ourselves groan within ourselves, waiting eagerly for our adoption as sons, the redemption of our body. (Romans 8:19-23)

The Gospel in Revelation

16. The eternal gospel has been understood as referring to the last gospel, the final gospel. This is the gospel during the time of judgment. The hour of judgment has come for the vindication of those who stay loyal to God despite adverse circumstances of persecution, coercion, and martyrdom.[5]

Already in Revelation 11:18 we were told "the time has come for judging the dead, and for rewarding your servants" (NIV). In this perspective, the three angels' messages are a last call for earth's people to repent and worship the Creator.

The gospel here is the one preached between the sixth and seventh trumpets.

The sixth trumpet ends with the acknowledgment that the rest of mankind, who were not killed by these plagues, did not repent of the works of their hands, so as not to worship demons, and the idols of gold and of silver and of brass and of stone and of wood, whichcan neither see nor hear nor walk; and they did not repent of their murders nor of their sorceries nor of their immorality nor of their thefts (Rev 9:20, 21).

At this point in salvation history, one could expect the sounding of the seventh trumpet and the consummation of salvation history; but what comes instead is an interlude, at the heart of which is the announcement to evangelize—in other words, to preach the gospel. Revelation 10 and 11 develop this theme.

---

[5] See James Nix, "A Unique Prophetic Movement," *Elder's Digest*, April/June 2015, 8-11.

17. Overall, the gospel is the good news of the liberation of God's people. This liberation is patterned after the liberation of Israel from Egypt and from Babylon.

18. The gospel is the good news of the judgment and fall of Babylon, announced in particular by the second angel's message. When God's people were informed that Babylon was fallen, it meant that they could go home.

19. The everlasting gospel is expressed in the three angels' messages, but there is more to the gospel than what is made explicit in them. Early Millerites and early Sabbatarian Adventists understood the three angels' messages in chronological sequence, but they finally came to adopt their interconnectedness and simultaneity. The first, second, and third messages came to be understood as inseparable. The everlasting gospel in its multifaceted dimensions is more comprehensive than what is made explicit in it in the three angels' messages.

20. The gospel is in the content of the three angels' messages. In other words, the everlasting gospel is contextualized in these messages. It has been argued that a key aspect of the gospel is the "righteousness of Christ" in the third angel's message. This is a key aspect of the gospel, but there are more dimensions both in the book of Revelation and in the rest of the Bible.

21. The gospel is the good news of the Second Coming of Jesus Christ, as described not only throughout the book of Revelation but notably right after the proclamation of the three angels' messages. The Second Coming is most certainly a crucial component of the gospel.

This aspect of the gospel is called the "blessed hope" (Titus 2:13).

22. The everlasting gospel is delineated contextually throughout the book of Revelation, including in the reversal of despair told in chapter 5, and in the vindication of the saints in the ushering in of justice.

A crucial element of the Good News: the restoration of justice.

- What the Lamb, who was slain and standing, secures is the restoration of a divine order of justice.

- "When he opened the fifth seal, I saw under the altar the souls of those who had been slain for the word of God and for the witness they had borne. They cried out with a loud voice, 'O Sovereign Lord, holy and true, how long before you will judge and avenge our blood on those who dwell on the earth?'

- "Then they were each given a white robe and told to rest a little longer, until the number of their fellow servants and their brothers should be complete, who were to be killed as they themselves had been" (Rev 6:9-11, ESV).

- The restoration of justice or vindication of martyrs is part of the good news and is a comfort to those loyal to Christ until death.

The good news is also expressed in chapter 7, where God's people, the servants and worshipers, are sealed.

The whole series of the seven seals then reveals several aspects of the good news. But the central work of redemption is the achievement of the cosmic Goel, or redeemer.

23. Contextually in the book of Revelation, the gospel is also articulated as God's victory in the great controversy. This victory's roots were fathomed in eternity. This may refer to the fact that God is not taken by surprise by evil, sin, or Satan and his allies, whether the third of the angels or the historical allies in the beasts from the land or from the sea (Rev 13).

24. Ultimately and in the highest sense, God is the everlasting good news. Only God is eternal. This understanding of the gospel is present from first chapter of the book. God is the One who is, who was, and who is to come. God is the one who provides freedom, grace, and peace, as told in the first chapter of the book.

A comprehensive understanding of the everlasting gospel is inseparable from God's self-revelation. As such, the gospel or good news is God's self-revelation in Christ through the Holy Spirit based on God's everlasting love. It is expressed through a New Covenant offered for the salvation of anyone who chooses to respond to the invitation of God's everlasting fellowship in love.

25. The gospel or good news is the announcement of the end of evil, the advent of total healing (Rev 22:2). There will no longer be any curse. The fatality of Eden will be completely reversed. There will be access to God. God's worshipers will see Him face to face, as He promised (Rev 22:4). Regency over creation will be restored.

26. In essence and in content, the gospel is the story of God. This is the story the book of Revelation tells. God's self-revelation in Jesus Christ is in fact the major subject matter of the book of Revelation.

God's self-revelation is expressed through the name of God, the gifts of God, the acts of God, and the sacrifice of Christ to secure the salvation of humankind. God invites the church and the whole human family to join God's story, God's acts for salvation, and God's fellowship.

Full fellowship with the Godhead is opened to those God created in His image for a covenant of fellowship in love. This overarching goal is the reason for the constitution of a kingdom of priests, the revelation of the divine dignity of the Son of Man, the High Priest in the midst of the seven lampstands—the church, the Lamb in the midst of God's throne, functioning like a cosmic Goel or redeemer.

All these designations and self-presentations of Christ show that God the Son is the good news, a way to say in apocalyptic language what was revealed in the Gospels:

"'This is My beloved Son, in whom I am well-pleased'" (Matt 3:17).